STORY

IN THE

STARS

STORY
IN THE
STARS

**DISCOVERING GOD'S DESIGN
AND PLAN FOR OUR UNIVERSE**

JOE AMARAL

New York   Nashville

FaithWords
Hachette Book Group
1290 Avenue of the Americas, New York, NY 10104
faithwords.com
twitter.com/faithwords

First Edition: October 2018

FaithWords is a division of Hachette Book Group, Inc. The FaithWords name and logo are trademarks of Hachette Book Group, Inc.

The publisher is not responsible for websites (or their content) that are not owned by the publisher.

The Hachette Speakers Bureau provides a wide range of authors for speaking events. To find out more, go to www.hachettespeakersbureau.com or call (866) 376-6591.

Library of Congress Control Number: 2018946513

ISBNs: 978-1-5460-1074-6 (trade paperback); 978-1-5460-1073-9 (ebook)

Printed in the United States of America

LSC-C

10 9 8 7 6 5 4 3 2

This book is dedicated to my wife, Karen. Of all the incredible, rare, amazing, and beautiful celestial objects in the universe, she outshines them all.

CONTENTS

CONTENTS

CONTENTS

CONTENTS

INTRODUCTION

In the beginning God created
the heavens and the earth.

—Genesis 1:1

TENS OF THOUSANDS of words have been written about the first ten words in the Bible: "In the beginning God created the heavens and the earth." Ten simple words that have ignited a firestorm of controversy and much debate. Since the dawn of time, people have endeavored to interpret and understand this opening statement of the Bible and learn the truth about our origins on this planet and in the universe.

It's absolutely amazing when you stop and think about it. We the human race have spent thousands of years trying to figure out this opening line of the Bible. It just goes to show you how much greater, grander, and wiser God is than us! It's no wonder there have been thousands upon thousands of books written about the Bible and about faith in general. If we get stumped on the first ten words, imagine the challenge of beginning to understand and decipher the remaining 783,127 words of Scripture.

What, Who, When, Where, or Why?

People generally get stuck on two questions about the opening verse of Genesis. The first question centers around the "when" of the text and the second is focused on the "how." When did God create the heavens and the earth? A quick internet search will produce a plethora of possibilities and theories.

For some, the earth was created approximately five thousand years ago. This number is based upon the names and genealogies that are found in the book of Genesis. It's definitely a possibility. The problem with this view is that you have to assume that Adam and Eve were created instantly and only five days after the creation of the universe. To be fair and reasonable, you have to account for the possible passing of time from when the earth was inhabitable for humans and from the time Adam took his first breath. Sure, only five days could have passed, but five eons could have also easily passed. This book by no means makes any attempt to settle the argument of the age of the universe, but the elephant in the room must be addressed.

For others, the earth was created billions of years ago. This, too, is a possibility. To better understand the Bible's opening statement, it's important to remember who wrote it. Its earthly author was Moses. This is almost an absolute certainty, as most scholars agree on Mosaic authorship. Who was Moses? When did he write this? Where was he when he wrote it? How did he get the information? These are very important questions that are seldom asked by the reader when trying to unravel the intricacies of the creation account. However, they are very important because they will help us establish a better framework of understanding.

Moses was the great leader of the Hebrew people, but we must remember where he spent the first part of his life: Egypt. There was nothing Hebraic or Jewish about Egypt. Being found and adopted by the pharaoh's daughter afforded him an incredible position that came with great prestige and privilege. The pharaoh at the time did not have a legitimate male child to take the throne after him. Moses, having been adopted into that family, became the legal heir to the throne. He would have received a pharaoh's education.

This means that Moses would have studied military tactics, ancient Near East philosophy, and religion. He would have learned mathematics, reading and writing, and, of course, astronomy and astrology. You don't have to dig too far into ancient Egyptian culture to discover that it was deeply steeped in astrology and religious mysticism. This belief system drove them to build the impressive and massive system of pyramids. It fueled their interest in the afterlife and what happened to the soul beyond the grave. We see this in the meticulous construction of the pharaohs' tombs and burial chambers.

Ancient Egyptian mythology has been preserved both in manuscripts and through hieroglyphics found in caves and chambers. Egyptology reveals a great curiosity about the cosmos and its creation. The ancient Egyptian god Khnum is said to have fashioned creation in the same manner as a potter fashions clay—slowly but surely molding and shaping the clay into the image or shape desired. This is very important information to consider when we are attempting to understand why Moses selected certain words over others in his creation account.

Strong's Concordance is the go-to concordance that Bible scholars use when they want to find the original Hebrew or Greek word and its meaning. The fifth word of the opening verse of the Bible is the word *created*. The Hebrew word used there is *bara* (see *Strong's* number H1254). It means "to shape, to form, or to fashion." The nuance of the word *bara* is not to create all at once but rather to set creation in motion. To fashion an object, and to take the time to perfect it.

Think of it this way. Even the tallest trees in the world—sequoias, a kind of redwood tree found in Northern California—grow to over 350 feet tall and yet begin with a seed that fits in the palm of your hand. Everything the tree would need over time was present at the very beginning.

So, too, in the beginning, everything that was necessary for the creation of the universe could have been present from the very start. Today it's known as the "Big Bang."

I know, I just lost some of you. You hear that term and you think it's a secular explanation for the beginning of the cosmos. But what if I told you that wasn't the case? What if I told you that, historically, the Big Bang Theory was a Christian perspective that was used to explain the beginning of space and time? In fact, in 1927, it was a Belgian Roman Catholic priest named Georges Lemaître, who was also an astronomer and physics professor, who noted the expansion of the universe. That is to say, he was the first to observe that deep-space objects such as galaxies were moving not only away from each other but from a single point in space. Lemaître's observations ultimately led to the theory known today as the "Big Bang."

Eventually, several other notable scientists and observable, empirical evidence corroborated his theory. Initially, the scientific community rejected Lemaître's theory because it confirmed the first three words of the Bible: "In the beginning." Before this theory, many in the world of science and cosmology hypothesized that the universe never had a beginning, that it had always existed. But this new evidence confirmed that there was a beginning, and that the Bible got it right. Somewhere along the journey, the term *Big Bang* became secular in nature. What was once a beloved discovery and victory for the church became a negative term, and those who declared faith in it were scorned as blasphemers and heretics. It's amazing what time can do. Time can heal all wounds, but it can also cause some of them.

It's a Big Universe

No matter which side of the spectrum you are on—young earth or old earth—we can all agree on the vastness of the universe. The truth is that we will never truly be able to understand how vast it really is. We can read all the facts and see all the pictures we want, but our human brains cannot fathom the reaches of the galaxy. We don't even understand the size of our planet, never mind the solar system. We can't even comprehend the size of our own star, the sun! How's this for some mind-blowing sun trivia: we could fit 1.3 million Earths inside of the sun! The sun makes up 99.86 percent of the total mass of the solar system, and yet it's called a "dwarf" yellow star. A dwarf! There are stars in the observable universe that are much, much larger than our own sun. For example, the largest detected star, to date, is VY Canis Majoris, which is Latin for "Big Dog." You could fit 9.3 billion of our suns in it! You can't even imagine it, can you? I know I can't.

NASA conservatively suggests there are anywhere from one hundred billion to four hundred billion stars in our Milky Way galaxy alone! That means there are about one hundred billion planets. It all seems so overwhelming. We hear these staggering numbers and our brain goes numb from trying to take it all in.

Let's start with something a little closer to home, something we may have a better chance of wrapping our heads around. Let's forget about the hundreds of billions of stars in the galaxy and focus on one: the nearest star to us. It's called Proxima Centauri, and it's a mere 4.22 light-years away. That doesn't sound too bad. Four is a small number. It should be fairly simple to understand its distance. Well...it doesn't sound like a lot, but of course, it is. That 4.22 light-years translates into forty trillion kilometers, or about twenty-five trillion miles. Some calculations suggest that at current rocket speeds, it would take us 137,000 years to get there, and that's just one way!

We haven't even left our own galaxy yet! Initially, NASA's Hubble Space Telescope estimated that there were approximately one hundred billion galaxies in the observable universe. But new data collected in 2016 by NASA now put that number at ten times greater—over one trillion galaxies! How's your head doing? My mind reels as I continue to research and discover more and more data about our universe. I'm trying, but I know I'm failing to convey how vast the universe really is.

So let's take another bite-sized look at things. We're unable to fathom hundreds of millions of galaxies, so let's look at just one. Let's look at the closest galaxy to us, Andromeda. It's considered to be the big-brother galaxy of the Milky Way. Our galaxy is 100,000 light-years wide, while Andromeda is approximately 220,000 light-years across—just over twice our size—yet it houses over a trillion stars, compared to our four hundred billion. Andromeda lies a mere 2.5 million light-years away from us, which, compared to the size of the universe, is right across the street. If we could travel at the speed of light, which is three hundred million meters per second, it would take us 2.5 million years to get there. Proxima Centauri at 137,000 years doesn't seem too far, does it?

The data above are precisely the reason why this is *not* a book about the when or how of creation. Hundreds of books on the subject have already been written by people who are much more qualified than I am. They are readily available, and if that area of research interests you, then go for it.

My area of interest and the focus and purpose of this book is to ask the question "Why?" Why create so many planets, stars, and galaxies? What purpose could they possibly serve? That's what I'll explore in the remaining pages of this book. Yes, we'll get theological and philosophical, but the answer is much simpler than all of that. The answer may surprise you. In fact, the answer *is* you! He made it all for you, and for me. As we will see, God went to extreme lengths to create, plan, and position all the heavenly bodies in the night sky. He did it to tell you a story. He placed a story in the stars—the story of faith, salvation, and redemption.

CHAPTER I

SIGNS

And God said, "Let there be lights in the vault of the sky to separate the day from the night, and let them serve as signs to mark sacred times, and days and years."

—Genesis 1:14

SOME SIGNS ARE region specific, while others are universal. I remember traveling through Australia in 2014 and seeing Kangaroo Crossing signs everywhere! That's an example of a region-specific sign. If you've seen them anywhere else, let me know. I've traveled to several countries around the world. I've been to Israel over forty times, and all throughout Southeast Asia, Europe, Mexico, and the UK, and it didn't matter which country I was in, I saw some universal signs. The most prominent was the stop sign. It didn't matter what language the sign was in. In fact, in some countries, there was no writing at all. As soon as I saw that red octagon, I instantly

STORY IN THE STARS

knew it was a stop sign. Not only did I recognize what the sign was, but I also knew what to do. I had to stop. That's it. No explanation or guidance was necessary. This is an example of an objective sign. You don't need to wonder about the meaning of a stop sign. The answer is clear and it is final.

Signs are put in place to either tell us something or point us toward something. A speed limit sign on the highway is an example of a sign that's there to tell us something. A sign on the highway may tell us to turn right up ahead because it's pointing us toward something, such as the destination that we have in mind.

That's exactly what God has done with creation. Genesis 1:14 tells us that God created the sun, moon, and stars to serve as signs. Just like natural signs, God's heavenly signs are there to tell us something and to point us toward something or, in this case, toward someone! God's signs are also objective. Later in this chapter we will be looking at whom these signs point to, but right now I want to address what the signs are and whom they are for.

You

As I said at the end of the Introduction, *you* are the reason God made the signs. He put them there because He loves you and He wanted to make sure that every single person who ever lived, no matter where or when, regardless of age or language, would be able to see and understand the signs. After all, the Bible says in 2 Peter 3:9b, "Instead he is patient with you, not wanting anyone to perish, but everyone to come to repentance."

His desire is and always has been for every single person who has ever lived to be in a right relationship with Him. He wants you to have eternal life. Having you with Him for all eternity is so important that He fashioned the entire universe to serve as a sign for you. Imagine that, if you can. Remember the massive universe I described in the introduction? Yeah, that one. He carefully created and planned it with extreme precision. He planned it to align with very specific dates and times throughout history.

Let's go back to the opening verse of Genesis 1:14. The "lights in the vault of the sky" described here refer to the sun, the moon, and the stars. They definitely serve a practical function. They divide the day from the night. They mark the days of the month. They basically serve as a celestial calendar. In ancient times, several cultures relied on the motion and phases of the moon to know when to plant and harvest their crops. But the text is telling us that they serve an even greater purpose. Unfortunately, we often miss this meaning because of the poor English translation.

A Word about Translation

English is a very restrictive and limited language when it comes to translating. As a person who comes from a

Portuguese background, I have seen this countless of times throughout my life. So often the original meaning is lost when translating from Portuguese to English or vice versa. This is what we see happening here.

The greater purpose that the sun, moon, and stars serve is to mark "sacred times." In English, it takes two words to convey the meaning of the original Hebrew word used in Genesis 1:14, which is *moed*. When read properly, the text tells us that the sun, moon, and stars serve as signs to mark *moeds*. So here's the million-dollar question: What in the world is a *moed*?

In Hebrew, *moed* refers to the holy days mentioned in the twenty-third chapter of the book of Leviticus in the Old Testament. The holy days are also known as the seven Feasts of the Lord. In our vernacular they are: Passover, Unleavened Bread, Firstfruits, Pentecost, Trumpets, Atonement, and Tabernacles. These seven annual festivals were instituted by God as holy or sacred times. Although the English translation gets the words right, it fails to convey the significance of the holy days and what they represent.

In essence, God said He would use celestial objects to serve as signs during these holy days. So it should be no surprise to see celestial signs during events like Passover or Tabernacles. They just show that God is doing exactly what He said He was going to do. As we will see, all throughout history, God has marked holy days with remarkable signs and wonders. For instance, to God, Passover is a sacred time, so He marks it with celestial activity: the first night of Passover is always marked by a full moon. This was so that the ancient Israelites would know exactly when the feast began.

Blood Moons

There was a lot of attention given to what the media called a tetrad of lunar eclipses during the years 2014 and 2015. These lunar eclipses are often referred to as "blood moons." This is how some of the ancient cultures described a lunar eclipse. The term has taken on an ominous association and meaning.

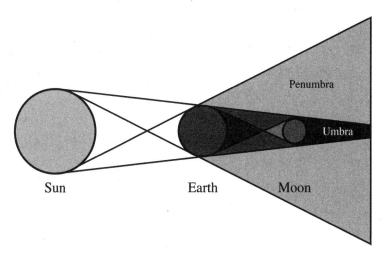

Lunar eclipse. *Illustration by Karen Amaral.*

As we all know, it takes the earth approximately 365 days to go around the sun once. During a lunar eclipse, the earth comes between the sun and the moon so that the moon receives no direct light from the sun; the earth is essentially blocking the incoming light that would normally give the moon the bright color we are used to seeing. During a *total* lunar eclipse, also known as a blood moon, the moon moves fully into the earth's shadow, which is called the umbra. The umbra gives off the earth's natural red hue. From our perspective, the moon transitions from the bright white we normally see to a reddish-orange color. If you've ever seen one, it's easy to understand why the ancients would refer to it as a "blood moon."

The blood moon tetrad of 2014–2015 garnered a lot of attention. Books were written. Documentaries were produced. Sermons were preached. The supposed common denominator of this tetrad, it was said, was that it was a rare phenomenon and carried with it a doomsday type of message. Surely it must have been a bad omen that marked imminent destruction. I don't know what year you are reading this book in, but I'm fairly confident that the world is still spinning, the sun is still shining, and life is going on as it has for some time now.

All people had to do was go back to Genesis 1:14. Of course there were blood moons during Passover and

Tabernacles—it's exactly what God said would happen. The danger of not having the Bible at the center of all our celestial interpretations is that we rely on human ideas. And as far as I am concerned, that's a very dangerous thing to do.

Blood moons and planetary alignments are normal and natural. That doesn't mean they're not special or important. More often than not, God uses the ordinary when creating the extraordinary. We see this throughout Scripture. Look back at the Exodus story of the Israelites. All ten plagues seem supernatural at first glance, but as we look at them more closely, we see that all God did was simply put His "super" on the "natural." From frogs to locusts to darkness, He used the nature that He had created for His purposes. That's precisely what we see with the sun, the moon, and the stars.

Jesus and the Zodiac

Blood moons and full moons have always occurred and will always occur during feast days because that's when they are supposed to happen. God's system to mark these days with celestial objects has been tested and proven with the passing of time. Even Jesus understood this principle. He talks openly about it in the Gospels, but somehow, we have missed it. We have been missing it for over two thousand years. It's now time to understand what He said and why. Consider the words of Jesus: "There will be signs in the sun, moon and stars" (Luke 21:25). Okay, I don't think you read that properly, so let's read it again. Jesus—the Messiah—said, "There will be signs in the sun, moon and stars."

I know you have read this before. I did, several times, as a seminary student during a Gospels course. I read it as a Bible teacher and as a pastor who had to prepare a new sermon every week. It wasn't until God, by the power of the Holy Spirit, opened my eyes and illuminated this passage to me that I began to understand. When I got ahold of what Jesus was saying and connected it to what God said in Genesis 1:14, it all started to come together. It was like this ancient, massive puzzle was starting to make sense. The pieces were literally falling into place. When Jesus said that the sun, moon, and stars would make a sign, it was like a gigantic lightbulb went off in my head. The signs He was speaking of were the constellations in the night sky!

What did He mean by this? Could God, can God, does God actually use the constellations for His purposes? As we continue through the various chapters in this book, we will see that God clearly designed and positioned the constellations in the night sky as part of the story that He has written in the stars. I know that idea may be challenging right now, and you might find it difficult to accept. But the verse in Luke is not a onetime mention in passing by Jesus. He says it more than once. In fact, the sacred Scriptures speak about it over and over again.

When Jesus was asked about the end times and what kind of signs we could expect, He answered in this way:

> Immediately after the distress of those days "the sun will be darkened, and the moon will not give its light; the stars will fall from the sky, and the heavenly bodies will be shaken." Then will appear the sign of the Son of Man in heaven. And then all the peoples of the earth will mourn when they see the Son of Man coming on the clouds of heaven, with power and great glory. (Matthew 24:29–30)

There is so much celestial activity going on in this passage that if we don't stop and think about it, we will miss it. Let's take a closer look at what He has mentioned here.

The first phenomenon He mentions is that the sun will be darkened. Before more recent times, with the advancement of science and research, many people believed that the signs in this passage were to be accomplished supernaturally. In a sense they are, because they have been designed by God. But in their truest sense, they're perfectly natural events. I say they're natural because they have been designed by God to operate in that way. This darkening of the sun is known as a solar eclipse. The most recent fully visible solar eclipse in the West was on August 21, 2017. Millions of Americans flocked into the streets to see this truly amazing celestial event.

A solar eclipse occurs when the moon passes between the sun and the earth and blocks the sun. I remember seeing video footage of the last solar eclipse from Nashville, Tennessee. It was amazing to see how dark it became in the middle of a sunny day, and how quickly it happened. This is exactly what Jesus was referring to in the Matthew passage. Now, a solar eclipse alone is not the sign of the end of all things. If you keep reading the passage, you will discover that several things need to occur at the same time.

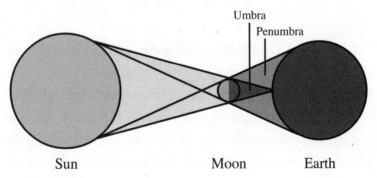

Solar eclipse. *Illustration by Karen Amaral.*

One more note about a solar eclipse: this can only happen on Earth. No other planet in our solar system was designed to have a solar eclipse. This is because of the size of our moon compared to the size of the sun, as well as the sun's distance from us. The diameter of the sun is approximately four hundred times larger than the diameter of the moon, and it is approximately four hundred times farther from us than the moon is. These conditions make it appear as if the sun and the moon are the same size in the sky. Some would suggest that this is simply a happy coincidence. Others, like myself, would suggest that it is too perfect to be accidental. It definitely screams intelligent design.

Shooting Stars

Jesus continues with three quick mentions of other celestial activity. First, He mentions that the moon will not give its light. This is a lunar eclipse, which we spoke about earlier. He then refers to the stars falling out of the sky. Stars in the sky are actually other suns in the galaxy. Our sun is also a star. Stars are fixed objects, meaning they don't move. Our sun is fixed. For centuries humans thought that the sun revolved around us, but with the advent of telescopes we quickly realized that it was the other way around. We revolve around a star. So, if stars are fixed in space, how can they move at all, let alone fall out of the sky?

Let me explain it this way. Have you ever been in a remote location? Perhaps on a camping trip or at a cottage far away from the bright city lights. The sky views are spectacular. The farther away you are from light pollution, the more objects you are able to see in the sky at night. We've all seen what we call a "shooting star." As a kid, I thought what I was seeing was exactly what the name suggested, that an actual star was falling out of the sky. We know this is impossible. Stars are millions and billions of times larger than the earth. If a star were actually "falling" from the sky, all life on the planet would be instantly wiped out. So what is it? What causes the streak in the sky that we call a shooting star?

The answer is a bit anticlimactic compared to a star actually colliding with our planet. Space is filled with incalculable amounts of debris. This debris is made of meteors, space rocks that range in size from a speck of dust to the size of a golf ball. As our planet orbits the sun, it runs into these rocks, which collide with our atmosphere at incredibly high speeds. When they travel though our upper atmosphere they begin to heat, glow, and then burn out. This is what happens when we see what we call a shooting star.

Because of the precision of our orbit around the sun, we always pass through the same region of space where comets have left behind a massive amount of debris. As we travel through it, we can see hundreds of fragments burning up in our atmosphere. This is what is known as a meteor shower. From our perspective, the stars appear to be falling out of the sky. So in the passage from Matthew above, we see that Jesus was referring to a meteor shower.

So He mentions a solar eclipse, a lunar eclipse, and now a meteor shower. What do we have involved here? The sun, the moon, and the stars. And He says that they serve as signs. That's exactly what He said in Luke 21:25 and what God said back in Genesis 1:14. He concludes the Matthew 24:29–30 passage by saying these objects will serve as the sign of the Son of Man. What objects in the sky are made up of these things? The constellations.

Let me give you just two examples of how the constellations have served as signs for the coming of the Son of Man. In fact, they continue to serve as signs to this very day—that's the nature of the stars. They were created to worship Him and reveal who He is. This is precisely what Nehemiah wrote about: "You alone are the LORD. You made the heavens, even the highest heavens, and all their starry host, the earth and all that is on it, the seas and all that is in them. You give life to everything, and the multitudes of heaven worship you" (Neh. 9:6).

If you stand outside on several clear nights in a row and look up at the night sky, you will notice a pattern. Every night is slightly different from the night before. It appears as if the stars and constellations are moving a bit farther apart each night. As we said earlier, stars don't move. The earth does. As we continue on our endless orbit around the sun, it gives the appearance that the stars are moving. Where we are on our orbit determines what we are able to see in the sky on any given night.

We take for granted what is in the sky each night. We assume the stars will be there, the moon will be there, and all will be as it should be. But have you ever taken the time to evaluate what stars are in the sky during certain seasons and, in turn, what constellations are in the sky? We know that Orion's Belt, for instance, is part of the greater winter constellation of Orion. What if the constellations in the sky are not random? What if specific constellations appear at the exact same time for all eternity on purpose?

Aries and Passover

Let's take two examples from the spring and autumn constellations. Every year during the months of March and April there is one dominant constellation in the sky: Aries. What is Aries? What figure represents this spring constellation? It's a ram. It has always been a ram. And it has always been in the night sky during this time of the year. At first you might say, okay, that's cool, but what does it have to do with worshipping God or pointing to the sign of the Son of Man? Aries in the night sky just happens to coincide with the Feast of Passover every year. Now, after all, God did say that the sun, moon, and stars would serve as signs to mark holy days and the feasts. Passover is the first feast mentioned in Leviticus 23.

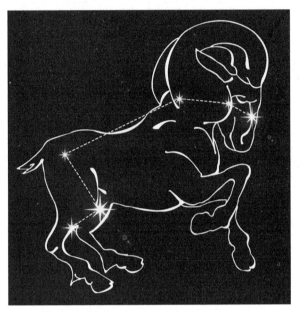

Constellation of Aries

Think about this. During the Exodus of the Israelites, God told Moses to slaughter a lamb, or ram. The blood was to be applied to the doorposts of Hebrew homes to serve as a sign for the angel of death. Go back even further, to the time of Abraham. God supplied a ram at Mount Moriah in Jerusalem as a substitute to die in the place of Isaac. These events happened in the spring. As they celebrated and commemorated these events on earth, Aries—the ram—was in the sky reminding the people of what God had done for them, that He had provided a sacrifice in the past and that He would ultimately provide the sacrifice to end all sacrifices.

Now fast-forward to the time of Jesus, who was called the Lamb of God in John 1:29 by John the Baptist and in Revelation 5:12–13. As Jesus, the Lamb of God, was being nailed to a tree as our Passover Lamb, Aries was in the sky, reminding both the ancients and us that the long-awaited Lamb had finally come . . . not just for them, but also for us. Next Passover, take the time to look up and you will see the sign of Aries in the sky, reminding you that Jesus—the Lamb of God—took our place and became our sacrifice.

As if all that wasn't enough . . . wait for it . . . there's more! Genesis 1:14 tells us that the sun, moon, and the stars not only mark feast days but are also used to mark days and years. In fact, as we will see, they were used to mark the birth, death, resurrection, and ascension of Jesus.

Astrology vs. Astronomy

Notice that I didn't mention the return of Jesus. That wasn't an oversight on my part. It was done on purpose and for a purpose. Constellational and planetary alignments should never be used in a predictive manner—meaning, don't try to figure out the future based on where the constellations and planets are. Not only is that nonsense, but it's also forbidden by God in several places throughout the Scriptures. It falls into the realm of astrology and borders on witchcraft. Deuteronomy 4:19 and Jeremiah 8:2 clearly command us to refrain from consulting and worshipping the sun, the moon, or the stars.

Let's take a closer look at the warning of Jeremiah 8:2: "They will be exposed to the sun and the moon and all the stars of the heavens, which they have loved and served and which they have followed and consulted and worshiped. They will not be gathered up or buried, but will be like dung lying on the ground."

Perhaps you're reading this right now and are wondering if this verse is still applicable today. After all, wasn't worship of the sun and idols a thing that was only done in the past? Are people still doing this today? Well, people may not be worshipping the sun, the moon, or the stars, but they are certainly consulting them. It's called astrology or, in modern-day nomenclature, horoscopes. Many people, including Christians, check their horoscopes every morning. They don't see any harm in it, or they think it's just something fun to read.

As we can see from this passage, consulting the stars is no laughing matter to God. He says that if you do so, you are like dung on the ground. Wow, that's a pretty vivid image. But what's so bad about astrology? The focus. People look to the stars and their positions in the night sky during certain months and rely on them for direction and counsel. Many people find their identity in their astrological sign. How many times have you heard people say something like, "That's such a Libra thing to do"?

The stars weren't created to counsel us or to speak to us about our lives. They were designed to reveal to us Jesus, who is the Bright Morning Star. We are to look to Him for counsel. It is in Christ and Christ alone that we find our identity. So don't get left behind like poop on the ground. Instead, fix your eyes on Jesus and look to the heavens for the sign of the Son of Man.

So then, we see that the heavenly alignments are reflective in nature, not predictive. We can look at key points in the life of Jesus and see how they were marked by celestial activity. But that activity should never be used to try to predict events—most of all, the return of Jesus.

Earlier, we noted Jesus' teaching about the celestial signs regarding the end times. A few verses later He confirms that we are not to try to predict or calculate when these things will occur. He puts it this way: "But about that day or hour no one knows, not even the angels in heaven, nor the Son, but only the Father" (Matt. 24:36).

So although we know that everything Jesus said will come to pass, we live in anticipation of those events without trying to pinpoint their exact dates or times.

Instead of trying to look forward, let's continue to look back and see how God marked the heavens when Jesus was crucified. As we do that, we see how God marked the death of Jesus during Passover in the sky. Not only was Aries present on the day of crucifixion, but another alignment took place in the same constellation that was nothing short of spectacular. But before we look at this amazing celestial event, it's important to determine the date of the crucifixion.

Date of Death

Our modern Good Friday celebration was established by the Roman emperor Constantine in the fourth century as the day to commemorate the crucifixion of Jesus. Different orthodox denominations celebrate it on various other days. The answer has eluded them all. The Scriptures are very clear about the date: Passover. That's it. No need for bizarre calculations or speculation. The Bible tells us it was Passover—plainly and simply.

Don't believe me? Believe Jesus. This is a direct quote from the Messiah Himself: "As you know, the Passover is two days away—and the Son of Man will be handed over to be crucified" (Matt. 26:2). When will He be handed over to be crucified? Passover. Here's another verse: "And he said to them, 'I have eagerly desired to eat this Passover with you before I suffer'" (Luke 22:15). What suffering was He referring to? The crucifixion. He was eating the customary Passover meal on the night before the lambs were sacrificed, called the Seder.

In Leviticus 23 we are told that Passover begins on the eve of Nissan 14, when you are to eat the meal. Nissan is the first month of the Hebrew religious calendar. The morning of the fourteenth day of Nissan was when the Passover lamb was to be sacrificed. So Jesus did as the Scriptures instructed. He ate the Passover meal with His disciples on the evening of the fourteenth, was arrested later that evening, and was crucified as the Lamb of God the very next morning.

How could it be the fourteenth of Nissan in the evening, when Jesus celebrated Passover *and* on the morning of the next day, when He was crucified? That's because, according to Genesis, a biblical day is from sunset to sunset. Therefore, it was the fourteenth for the meal and still the fourteenth for the crucifixion.

So we know Jesus was crucified during Passover, but how can we know which year it was and what day of the week it was? Those are great questions. Thankfully, God did what He said He would do. He marked the crucifixion with celestial activity.

In order to arrive at the date, we look to the text to tell us what happened in the heavens the day He was crucified. Matthew 27:45 tells us that "from noon until three in the afternoon darkness came over all the land." That's a pretty remarkable and clear celestial sign. If total darkness covered the land for three hours, then we should expect there was a solar eclipse, but historically we know that didn't occur. Nor did it need to. Again, if we simply read the text, it speaks for itself.

Solar Eclipse vs. Lunar Eclipse

In the original language, the Bible didn't say there was total or complete darkness, just darkness. That may not sound like a big difference, but it completely alters our understanding of what took place in the sky that day. As we research the original language, we find that the word used for darkness in this text is the Greek word *skotos*, which comes from another Greek word, *skia*. This word literally means "shade caused by the interception of light." Notice that *shading* of light occurred—not complete darkness. With this understanding, it sounds more like a lunar eclipse, which is caused when the earth comes between the sun and the moon and intercepts the light.

So a solar eclipse didn't mark Jesus' crucifixion but rather a lunar eclipse. Thanks to modern astronomy software and an online database archive, we have a date when this occurred. NASA confirms that on April 3, AD 33 (according to our modern-day Gregorian calendar), a partial lunar eclipse took place that lasted for two hours and fifty minutes. This seems to match and fit the three-hour description of the Gospels.

Let's do a quick recap before we move into the next

celestial sign during Jesus' crucifixion. Jesus was crucified on the morning of Passover; during His crucifixion
a lunar eclipse took place and the constellation of Aries
was in the sky. Does this sound familiar? Remember when
we began in Genesis 1:14? God said He would use the sun,
the moon, and the stars (or constellations) to serve as
signs to mark the holy days. I love how God is always right
on the money—not just close or approximate but 100 percent accurate and on time.

With the use of astronomy software, we can go back
to April 3, AD 33, and see exactly what the sky looked in
Jerusalem on the day of the crucifixion. At 3 p.m., when

Sun under the foot of Aries

the Gospels say Jesus died, there was a lunar eclipse rising over Jerusalem and Aries was in the sky as the sun was passing through it. At 3 p.m., the sun was under the foot of Aries—a clear and moving sign that the Son, who was the Lamb, was being crushed.

This is what Jesus referred to when He said there would be signs with the sun, moon, and stars. This is also what He meant when He said we would see the sign of the Son of Man in the heavens. Remarkable. Absolutely remarkable. No wonder the prophet said, " 'For my thoughts are not your thoughts, neither are your ways my ways,' declares the LORD. 'As the heavens are higher than the earth, so are my ways higher than your ways and my thoughts than your thoughts' " (Isa. 55:8–9).

Aquarius and Tabernacles

The first example of a constellation that we looked at that coincided with an event in the life of Jesus was Aries during Passover. A second example involves the constellation Aquarius, whose name means "water carrier." You've probably heard of this one and already know what image is used for this sign. Aquarius is always represented by a man holding a jug that is spilling water into the mouth of the fish in the constellation Piscis Austrinus in the southern hemisphere. Let's see how God used this sign to mark a feast day and a significant event in the life of Jesus.

Constellation of Aquarius

To make this connection, we will turn our attention to a story that is recorded in John 7:37: "On the last and greatest day of the festival, Jesus stood and said in a loud voice, 'Let anyone who is thirsty come to me and drink.'" A powerful portion of Scripture. To make the connection between the sign of Aquarius and John 7:37, some cultural background significantly helps in understanding the relation between the two. The first thing to identify in this passage is what is going on culturally. John mentions a festival. He doesn't name it, but he makes a remark that is a dead giveaway if you understand the religious cycle of the people living at that time.

John remarks that Jesus makes this statement "on the last and greatest day of the festival." According to Leviticus 23, there is only one festival that has a "last and greatest day": the celebration of Tabernacles. There were unique ceremonies that took place each day during this festival, but it culminated with a special ceremony on the last day that was not only spectacular, but it was also unforgettable.

The priest would leave the temple area carrying an empty jug. That's interesting. He would go down to an area called the Pool of Siloam, a spring-filled pool used for ritual cleansing. There are only three sources for living water: rain, rivers, and springs. Because it was spring-fed, it qualified as a source of living water. The priest would dip the empty jug into the Pool of Siloam and fill it to the brim with this living water. He would then carry it back to the temple courts, where, during the ceremony, he would spill the water out onto the altar.

The Feast of Tabernacles takes place in the fall, during late September and early October. It's the final of the seven feasts mentioned in the Old Testament. The land of Israel would have just gone through the dry season (the rains would start in November), so it would not have rained for several months leading up to this event. The pouring out of the water was a symbolic gesture. It was an outward sign of an inner prayer request for God to send the winter rains. As already mentioned, rain was a form of living water—in fact, it was the purest of the three. So as the people were praying and asking for living water, Jesus appeared in the temple, right on cue.

Earlier in John, the Bible says that Jesus timed his departure from Galilee to arrive in Jerusalem at the precise time the request for living water was being made. When He made the claim to be the living water that people were looking for, the connection was obvious to everyone there. As the sun began to set over Jerusalem, the stars began to shine. Just imagine it. With zero light pollution two thousand years ago, the sky would have been dazzling and bursting with stars. As the festival was coming to a close, people saw the priest with a jug pouring out water, and Jesus made the claim to be the living water. In the sky, at that exact moment, was the constellation of Aquarius, pouring out his living water into the mouth of the fish! The timing was impeccable. Only God could do such a thing.

As we close this chapter, let us remind ourselves why the sun, the moon, and the stars were created: they serve as signs, both then and now. Whether it was Aries in the sky during Passover or Aquarius in the sky during Tabernacles, these constellations marked not only the holy days but also significant events in the life of Jesus. God did all this because He wants everyone to know who His Son is—that Jesus is the promised Messiah. That Jesus is the one who died for our sins. That Jesus is the one who can restore and refresh our souls with His living water.

The next chapter will encourage you as you see how God went to incredible lengths to create and position the universe to tell the story of His salvation. But before we get there, let me leave you with this reminder from Scripture: "They know the truth about God *because he has made it obvious to them.* For ever since the world was created, people have seen the earth and sky. Through everything God made, they can clearly see his invisible qualities—his eternal power and divine nature. So they have no excuse for not knowing God" (Rom. 1:19–20 NLT, emphasis mine).

He wanted you to know Him. So He placed a story of epic proportions in the stars.

Chapter 2

LISTEN CLOSELY

The heavens declare the glory of God;
the skies proclaim the work of his hands.
Day after day they pour forth speech;
night after night they reveal knowledge.
They have no speech, they use no words;
no sound is heard from them.
Yet their voice goes out into all the earth,
their words to the ends of the world.

—Psalm 19:1–4

IN THE FIRST chapter, we spent some time developing the idea that God's plan for the constellations was that they would serve as signs. They marked feast days and important dates and events in the life of Jesus the Messiah. In this chapter, as the old saying goes, we're gonna up the ante. Not only was it God's desire to use the constellations as signs, but He also specifically designed them to point to one incredibly important fact.

Consider the words of 1 Corinthians 15:41: "The sun has one kind of splendor, the moon another and the stars another; and star differs from star in splendor." Remember the hundreds and hundreds of trillions of stars mentioned in the introduction? Well, according to this verse, although God created and named them all, some of them serve a more noble purpose. The text says that some stars differ from other stars in splendor, that is, in importance.

Cosmologists tell us that every star serves a purpose. The gravitational pull of one star will affect another nearby star system. Even when a star explodes and goes supernova, it expels necessary gases and chemicals into space that assist in the birth of new stars and galaxies. It also means that some stars are more noble than others in that they are the ones chosen to form the outlines of the various constellations.

The Heavens Declare

But wait, there's more. The psalmist penned one of the most famous phrases in the entire Bible. Some of you may even have these words framed and hanging somewhere in your home or office. As you should—it's a dynamic and powerful piece of Scripture. But, like many verses, there's more to the story. Here's the piece of Scripture I'm referring to: "The heavens declare the glory of God; the skies proclaim the work of his hands. Day after day they pour forth speech; night after night they reveal knowledge. They have no speech, they use no words; no sound is heard from them. Yet their voice goes out into all the earth, their words to the ends of the world" (Ps. 19:1–4).

It's such a popular and beautiful piece of biblical literature that even the apostle Paul quoted it in the New Testament. He used it to make a point of how everyone has had the opportunity to hear the message of the gospel. This is what he wrote:

How, then, can they call on the one they have not believed in? And how can they believe in the one of whom they have not heard? And how can they hear without someone preaching to them? And how can anyone preach unless they are sent? As it is written: "How beautiful are the feet of those who bring good news!" But not all the Israelites accepted the good news. For Isaiah says, "Lord, who has believed our message?" Consequently, faith comes from hearing the message, and the message is heard through the word about Christ. But I ask: Did they not hear? Of course they did: "Their voice has gone out into all the earth, their words to the ends of the world." (Romans 10:14–18)

Paul was dealing with an issue that we still face in our culture today. The question was, what happens to the people who never hear the message of the gospel? I'm sure you've heard this, too; we all have. Earlier, I pointed us to Romans 1:19–20, where Paul writes that no one can give the excuse of not knowing or seeing God. He states that the sky—that is, the heavens, the sun, the moon, and the stars—are enough to show a person that there is a God. He's essentially saying the same thing here, but this time he employs a well-known passage from the Old Testament. Let's look at the passage of Psalm 19:1–4 and see how Paul uses it to build his case for creation being enough to lead people to salvation. It's a very powerful and well-thought-out presentation.

Everyone knows the first line: "The heavens declare the glory of God." End statement. Sadly, this is where most people stop when reading this passage, but there is more, so much more. Also, why does the apostle include this Old Testament quote in a message in which he is dealing with salvation by observing nature, namely the sky? That's because people of that time knew something that we didn't. They were also able to see things that we could not see. I'm not just referring to spiritual things but to natural things.

Can you imagine what the night sky looked like two thousand years ago? There was zero light pollution. The stars and constellations would have been not just visible but pronounced. Their shapes would have been easier to make out in the sky. The words from the psalm are remarkable. Even if you just take them at face value, they are beautiful and poetic. But let's take a closer look at the phrasing used by the psalmist. He starts by saying that the heavens "declare." That the skies "proclaim." Then he says that they "pour forth speech" and that they "reveal knowledge."

So far, every verb and phrase used suggests that words are involved in declaring the glory of God. Whatever the glory of God is, it's so important that all of creation speaks to it. Later in this chapter we will reveal what the glory of God actually is, but for now, let's focus on the word selection here.

The first half of the passage has, in some form or another, the heavens talking or speaking about God's glory. Then, partway through the passage, the writer takes a sharp turn and completely changes the way he writes and the words he uses. Now he says, "they have no speech" and "no sound is heard from them." The language used here is a big departure from the first part of the passage. In the first few lines, the heavens are proclaiming, declaring, and revealing. In the second half, they give us the silent treatment and don't utter a single word.

So that's pretty confusing. But wait, it gets more confusing. Then the psalmist says that their voice and words go out into all the earth. Hang on. Is it just me or does that sound a little contradictive? How can something say something about something without saying anything? (Did you follow that?) It's only confusing or contradictory if you fail to make an ancient connection. People from that time often used nonverbal communication as a means to convey a message.

A Picture-Perfect Sky

What is in the sky every night? The moon and the stars. Building on what we talked about earlier, noble stars are used to outline the figures of the constellations. Some of them include Virgo, Aries, Aquarius, and Leo. Why in the world I would mention these signs at this time? Well, we already saw how Aries and Aquarius were present at key moments in Jesus' life and death. If God has used these two, could He use—and has He used—the other ten? Of course He has. Think of it this way: How do you tell a story or share information without using a single word? That's easy: pictures!

Long before writing emerged as the most popular way of communication, there were pictures. Whenever archaeologists find a cave from five thousand years ago or more, they seldom find writing in it, but they almost always find drawings or pictures. What's that old adage? "A picture is worth a thousand words." In this case it is especially true.

Let me illustrate it this way. Suppose you went into a room that had four pictures on the wall. No words, no writing, no captions, just images. The first image is of a man. So far, so good. The second image is of a lion. I think we're still pretty clear. The third image is of the lion chasing the man. I think we can see where the story is going. The fourth and final image is of a pool of blood. Gruesome, I know, but it illustrates the ending pretty well. You see, with just four images, we told an entire story—the lion killed the man.

Now, let's apply that logic to the constellations in the night sky. There are twelve constellations rotating throughout the heavens, year after year, millennia after millennia. It is the greatest picture show in the universe. Like a massive PowerPoint presentation, the heavens are declaring and proclaiming the glory of God. They use no words, they don't make a sound, but night after night, they reveal knowledge about the glory of God. So what is the glory of God? Because, whatever it is, the entire universe was designed to reveal it. I think that is the wrong question. You see, the glory of God is not a "what" but rather a "who." Who is the glory of God?

The answer, as always, can and should be found in the Scriptures. And so it is. "The Son is the radiance of God's glory and the exact representation of his being" (Heb. 1:3). Jesus is the glory of God, and all of creation exists to reveal who He is! That means that every star

42

and every constellation in the night sky was put there by God to point us to His Son. Incredible. Only the God of creation could do such a thing. Every constellation in the zodiac paints for us a different scene from the life of Jesus. From the virgin birth in Virgo to the returning and conquering King in Leo and everything in between, it's all there. It has always been there and it will always be there. Because God loves us so much and wants us to know Him, He has created, designed, and arranged the universe in order to tell us a story in the stars.

God's plan from the very beginning was that the world would know that Jesus was the Messiah and Savior of the world. It was so important that He literally moved heaven and earth to reveal Him. In 1 Peter 1:20, it's put this way: "He was chosen before the creation of the world, but was revealed in these last times for your sake." How has He been revealed? How are those living today, who never met or saw Him, to know who He is? In short, the answer is the heavens. They declare and reveal the glory of God, who is Christ. Day after day, night after night, He is being revealed through the constellations in the sky. But are we listening?

Origins

Now, you might be asking who named the constellations and designed the shapes in the sky. You might also be asking how it's possible that every major civilization since the dawn of time has always seen the exact (and when I say exact, I mean the same exact) forty-eight constellations. If you or I were to look up at the sky tonight, I doubt we'd be able to make out the shape of a bull, a centaur, or a scale. So how did the shapes and images come into being? It's a great question.

First of all, the original word for *constellation* in the Bible is the Hebrew word *Mazzaroth*. It's only used once in the entire Scripture and has a very specific and unique meaning. To quote *Strong's Concordance*, word number H4216 means "the twelve signs of the Zodiac and their thirty-six associated constellations." We will spend lots of time talking about the forty-eight signs of the constellations and their connections to Christ in the next chapter, but right now, I want to show you, from Scripture, that God takes sole responsibility for creating and naming the Mazzaroth—that is, the constellations and/or signs of the zodiac.

The only time the word *Mazzaroth* is ever used is in the Book of Job. God says in response to Job, "Can you bind the chains of the Pleiades? Can you loosen Orion's belt? Can you bring forth the constellations in their seasons or lead out the Bear with its cubs?" (Job 38:31–32). Mentioned in this portion of Scripture are two iconic celestial objects: the Pleiades cluster of seven stars in the constellation of Taurus, and Orion's Belt, from the Orion constellation. Scholars suggest that the Book of

Job is one of the oldest, if not the oldest, piece of literature in all of human history, spanning back some six thousand years. Think of it. Six thousand years ago, people already knew the names of the constellations. That's absolutely incredible.

But how did we get the names and shapes of the forty-eight constellations? Who got to decide which stars to use and which shapes to make? I suppose one could ask the same question of all the trees, plants, and animals. God ultimately made the decision to entrust the responsibility to Adam. It seems that He may have done the same thing with the constellations. At least, this is what has been handed down to us from one of the greatest historians of all time: Flavius Josephus. He was born in AD 37 and was an eyewitness to the destruction of the temple in Jerusalem in AD 70.

At this point it's important to stress what a reliable historian Josephus really was. His books are considered sacred in the world of archaeology; many swear by the accuracy of his writings. Villages that were lost for two thousand years have been found because archaeologists followed the directions of Josephus. Parts of King David's palace and other sacred spaces have been discovered because of the incredible detail Josephus used to describe their original locations from antiquity. Josephus is not only credible but also very reliable.

His two main works are *History of the Jewish War* and

Antiquities of the Jews. As the name suggests, *History of the Jewish War* is a detailed chronology of the conquests of the Roman Empire, specifically in the regions of Israel and the rest of the Middle East. *Antiquities of the Jews* contains a fairly detailed account of the history of the Jewish people. One of the unique features of his writings is the preservation of oral history—that is, Jewish tradition. Much of what had been passed down from generation to generation was in oral form. A lot of history occurred before writing became the main means of communication. To this day, rabbis grant much authority to the information that was passed down orally. This is very important for us because Josephus makes a fascinating remark regarding, of all things, the origin of astronomy!

There is almost no mention at all in historical records of the origins of astronomy. The only source I've been able to find is by Josephus. Consider what he wrote in *Antiquities of the Jews*, book 1, chapter 3, verse 69b: "They also were the inventors of the peculiar sort of wisdom which is concerned with the heavenly bodies, and their order." Who is he writing about here? Whoever it is, Josephus seems to be crediting them as the first to chart the movements of the stars and constellations. You may be surprised to learn that he is speaking of a man named Seth and his descendants. That's right, Seth— the third son of Adam and Eve. If you'll recall the story, the first two children of Adam and Eve were Cain and

Abel. Cain killed Abel and was banished from the Garden of Eden.

Genesis tells us that a third son was born to Adam and Eve some time later, and his name was Seth. If Josephus is correct in preserving this oral tradition—and we have no reason to doubt him—then it is possible that Adam shared knowledge of the constellations with his son Seth. In whatever manner Seth came to understand the motions and patterns of the heavenly bodies, the earliest Jewish sources credit him as one of the first celestial observers.

Supporting what Josephus wrote, there are some early Hebrew, Persian, and Arabian traditions that credit the invention of astronomy to Adam, Seth, and Enoch, respectively. There are even some scholars who suggest that the signs of the zodiac, or Mazzaroth, and the names of the stars that form their images originally were created as a mnemonic device by these forefathers of the Hebrews to tell the story of the Bible. The apocryphal Book of Jubilees states, "And he [Enoch] was the first among men that are born on earth who learnt writing and knowledge and wisdom and who wrote down the signs of heaven according to the order of their months in a book, that men might know the seasons of the years according to the order of their separate months."

Another apocryphal book, the Book of Enoch, devotes much text to the movements of celestial objects.

It's important to note here that we have examples of many ancient cultures that were not only fascinated with astronomy but also understood its importance and value. The term used to describe this kind of study is *archaeoastronomy*. (Don't worry, that's the only big word I'll use in this book.) It shouldn't surprise us that the ancient Hebrews preserved this celestial knowledge. In fact, we should be extremely thankful. Much of the information we have today about the origins of the constellations comes to us from them.

A Backyard Astronomer

All over the world, telescopes are pointed up toward the heavens. Mankind has spent billions and billions of dollars in order to get a better view and a better understanding of what is out there. The Hubble Space Telescope, launched in 1990, was a game changer that literally allowed us to peer into the outskirts of the observable universe. Billions and billions of stars and galaxies have since been discovered. It let us to look into nebulas and star clusters. We've been able to glean more information about star formation and their effects on other celestial bodies, and we've seen images of deep space that are mesmerizing and haunting at the same time.

The Hubble had an initial cost of $1.5 billion. NASA's James Webb Space Telescope hovered around the $10 billion mark. If it will be able to do just half of what we have been told, then we are in for one exhilarating ride! Then there's the single most expensive joint project in the history of humanity: the International Space Station. This incredible piece of human ingenuity set us back $150 billion in 1998 and will be in operation until 2028.

All of this money and effort is the human attempt, knowingly or unknowingly, to understand the first ten words of Genesis: "In the beginning, God created the heavens and the earth." God spoke the cosmos into existence, and we have been desperately trying to comprehend how it all works. Some of humanity's greatest minds have given us insight into how the universe functions, yet we are far from understanding some of the most basic elements of our own planet. We understand that we have a solar system made of planets and their respective moons. We understand how planets orbit the sun. We understand that there exists an incredible balance in the universe that is so finely tuned the slightest cosmic alteration would have prevented life from existing. Yet for all our knowledge, for all the money we have spent and for all the adventures we have embarked on, we still have more questions than we do answers.

At first glance, the orbits of the planets in our solar system seem to be quite random. We know how long each planet takes to make one orbit around the sun. For instance, our planet, Earth, takes 365 days to make one trip around the sun. Mercury, the closest planet to the sun, does it in just 88 days. Neptune, the farthest planet, does it in a whopping 165 years. If we were to ever reinstate poor Pluto as a planet, then we could mention that it takes an incredible 248 years to make just one trip around the sun.

Because of the various lengths of time that the planets take to orbit the sun, we often have planetary alignments, which are also known as conjunctions. They happen all the time. They're a spectacular sight. What's very cool about this is that most of them can be seen with the naked eye. They can appear to be one massive or bright star, but if you were to observe them through a telescope, you would see that there is more than one planet or another celestial object present. This is what occurred on the night of Jesus' birth, which we will look at in great detail in chapter 4. While NASA and other space agencies have spent billions of dollars to gaze at the stars, one person with a backyard telescope captured a comet slamming into one of our planets, which occurred during a very significant time of the year.

While to some the planetary orbits and alignments can seem ordinary and random, we have biblical evidence to the contrary. In fact, the Bible says that there is great purpose in the positioning and alignment of the stars and planets. Look at what it says in Psalm 8:3–4: "When I consider your heavens, the work of your fingers, the moon and the stars, which you have set in place, what is mankind that you are mindful of them, human beings that you care for them?"

Although we can observe and explain how the planets orbit around the sun, there is absolutely nothing we can do to manipulate or affect their orbits in any way. All we can do is watch and wait. Not so with God. According to what we just read in Psalm 8:3, God, and God alone, has determined the positions and movements of the planets. The comet impact that I referred to earlier is a perfect example of God's providence concerning planetary alignments. Allow me to explain.

With the naked eye, or even with a telescope, we can't see all the planets at once to determine where they are on their orbital paths. But due to the infinite precision with which the planets move, we can extrapolate their exact positions. A quick internet search will produce a plethora of websites with animations of planetary motions. They're fun to watch. Because of its proximity, you'll see Mercury whipping around the sun and you'll observe Neptune crawling along its orbit. As all the planets move in their respective orbits, you will notice that from time to time, they align with each other. In and of itself, this is not an amazing happening. What is amazing, however, is when specific planets align at specific times with other planets in a protective role.

Think of the planets in our solar system as a family. Just like a human family, the planets look out for each other. We have examples of larger planets coming between a smaller planet and a large asteroid, preventing catastrophic damage. Asteroids and comets slam into moons and planets all the time. It's usually not that big a deal. But every now and then, an extinction-level celestial bad boy enters our solar system and causes massive damage. Some have theorized this may have caused a global calamity and the subsequent dinosaur extinction. So what if planetary orbits aren't random? What if there is a plan and a purpose to their timing and positions? Let's explore the family analogy a bit further. If Mercury represents the baby of the family, then the other planets represent the other siblings in the family. In this case, then Jupiter, without a doubt, would be the big brother. It's natural for the big brother to watch out for and protect his smaller siblings. I'm a big brother, and if you want to mess with my little brother or sister, you have to get through me first. This is precisely the behavior we see in planetary orbits.

An Explosive Encounter

In keeping with my family analogy, in ancient times, the Assyrians referred to the stars as soldiers serving the God of heaven. In some ancient Jewish traditions, the rabbis would often refer to the planets as kings. This being the case, and it being the largest of the planets, Jupiter would be referred to as the king of kings. This comes as no

Jupiter, the King Planet

shock to us. Even to this very day, groups like NASA refer to Jupiter as the King Planet. It's an easy and justifiable identification.

Something happened on March 17, 2016, between Jupiter and an incoming comet. What's really exciting about this encounter is that it was caught on tape! Earlier, I mentioned that an amateur astronomer caught a comet slamming into one of our planets with his backyard telescope. I encourage you to look it up online.

At first glance, it doesn't look like much. In fact, it's pretty unimpressive when you first watch it. You can see Jupiter hovering in the center of the screen, and then at the middle-right edge of the planet, a little white blip occurs. It's quite bright but lasts only for a moment. You'll have to watch it a few times to really see it.

No one paid attention to it at first. A space rock hit Jupiter. Big whoop, right? That's what astronomers thought when they first heard about the impact. To be honest, because of Jupiter's size, it's not uncommon for it to be struck by meteors or comets. Astronomers did their due diligence and watched the footage. They were absolutely blown away by what they saw. The velocity at which the comet crashed into Jupiter caused an explosion that was equivalent to many millions of atomic bombs.

Upon analyzing the blast, they determined that the size of the impact ring left by the space crash was the same size as Earth. If that comet had somehow made its way through the inner solar system and slammed into Earth, it would have been what astronomers call a biosphere-changing event. In simple terms, we would not be here. To call it catastrophic would be to put it mildly.

Think of all the tiny and seemingly insignificant steps that had to occur in order for the comet to hit Jupiter and no other planet or moon. It's almost incalculable. Just think about all the details that had to happen and be in the right place. And all of them would have to be unplanned. They had to occur naturally. No design. No purpose. Just dumb luck. Jupiter was in the exact perfect position to receive the impact. The comet entered into the solar system on the right day and traveled on the right course at the right speed and at the right angle. Jupiter's moons were out of the way (and that's saying something, since there are sixty-seven of them). Jupiter was far enough from Earth on its orbit that it caused no collateral damage to us or to any other planet. Jupiter's gravitational pull was just strong enough to pull in the comet and take the impact. Does it still sound like a happy space accident to you? Nah. Me neither.

But wait. You guessed it, there's more. There's so much more. Think about all the terminology that has been used to describe the Jupiter impact. The king of kings took upon itself the pain of the impact and was pierced by the comet. The planet was bruised and stricken. I'm fighting back tears as I write this. Can there be a more powerful picture in the heavens of what Jesus, the King of Kings, has done for us? At this point, we have to read what the prophet Isaiah wrote about the coming Messiah, about what He would go through on our behalf: "Surely he took up our pain and bore our suffering, yet we considered him punished by God, stricken by him, and afflicted. But he was pierced for our transgressions, he was crushed for our iniquities; the punishment that brought us peace was on him, and by his wounds we are healed" (Isa. 53:4–5).

Remember what it says in Psalm 19? "The heavens declare the glory of God." And remember how we said that the glory of God wasn't a "what" or a thing but a "who"? And that Hebrews 1:3 says, "The Son is the radiance of God's glory and the exact representation of his being." So in this planetary impact, we see that on March 17, 2016, the heavens were reminding us that Jesus, the Son and glory of God, the King of Kings, took upon Himself the punishment that we deserved.

I'm reminded of how Psalm 19 also says that night after night, the heavens are pouring forth speech and revealing knowledge about the glory of God without uttering a single word. This kind of space collision is precisely what this verse is referring to. You see, Jupiter didn't say a word. The comet that slammed into Jupiter didn't say a word. But if we are willing to see the signs, the heavens were screaming that night. And what were they screaming? They were saying that God loves us so much that He sent His one and only Son to take our punishment. If that ain't love, then I don't know what love is.

Timing Is Everything

If all that weren't enough, there's still one more thing about the impact of March 17, 2016, that I'd like to share with you. Where was Jupiter, the king of kings, on the day of the impact? After all, if God did design the universe to reflect His plan of salvation, then it would come as no surprise if there was either a unique planetary alignment or significant constellation in the sky during that time. In fact, both occurred. To my utter amazement, Jupiter, the King Planet, was directly under Leo, the constellation of the king and royalty. But not only was Jupiter under Leo, it was also under his paw. At 8:17 p.m. EST, at the exact moment of the impact, Leo was literally trampling on Jupiter—an incredible symbol of the sacrificial life of Jesus. The Lion willingly allowed Himself to be pierced, bruised, and striped for us!

One last side note: the impact occurred between two sacred Jewish feasts, Purim and Passover. Purim is a holiday that commemorates the day that God saved His people from complete annihilation at the hands of Haman and the wicked Persian Empire. Passover commemorates the day that God saved His people from the angel of death by sacrificing a lamb on their behalf. And to top it all off, Aries—the constellation that represents sacrifice—was in the sky that night. Isn't it just like God to place these signs in the heavens to remind us that He has truly written a story in the stars?

CHAPTER 3

PICTURE THIS

Can you bring forth the constellations in their seasons?

—Job 38:32

IN THE PREVIOUS chapter, I threw out the names of some constellations. You may have missed them because their mention was so brief. I did that on purpose, to introduce you to the concept of some of the signs of the zodiac before we begin to deep dive into them in this chapter. Some of you might be going back to the previous line because you saw a word that you're not used to seeing within a Christian context: "zodiac." Yes, I said the Z word. Most Christians have hesitancy in their hearts about even saying the word, let alone studying what it means.

Let me stress that when I use the term *zodiac* in this book, I am just referring to the ancient name given to the collection of constellations. It is in no way an endorsement or recognition of the modern-day pseudoscience of astrology. God warns and commands us not to consult the stars for personal gain or benefit.

While we're on the subject, let's address another misconception. Some people feel that looking at any of the images of the zodiac is wrong because they were created by the enemy. I understand the confusion. You see, the enemy did not create the sun, the moon, or the stars. The enemy did not name and position them. God did all that. We already established this when we saw it in Job 38:31–32. All the enemy has done, and is ever able to do, is to distort and twist what God has created. It started in the Garden of Eden and it continues to this very day. God takes full responsibility and credit for both creating and maintaining the zodiac, but it has definitely been hijacked by the world and the enemy. It was never meant to mean what it means today. The online Oxford Living Dictionaries simply defines *zodiac* as "a belt of the heavens within about eight degrees either side of the ecliptic, including all apparent positions of the sun, moon, and most familiar planets. It is divided into twelve equal divisions or signs (Aries, Taurus, Gemini, Cancer, Leo, Virgo, Libra, Scorpio, Sagittarius, Capricorn, Aquarius, Pisces)." *Zodiac* derives from the Latin word *zōdiacus* and the Greek word *zōidiakòs* and refers to the cyclic or circular apparent movement of an object.

Notice the term "apparent movement." It's a small detail but a very important one. If you've ever observed the sky over several nights or months, you'll notice that the stars and constellations seem to move. For instance, right now where I live, Orion is a prominent constellation in the sky. It's very easy to identify because of the famous asterism, Orion's Belt. An asterism isn't in and of itself a constellation, but it's an image or pattern formed by stars within a constellation. The most famous one in the northern hemisphere is the Big Dipper, which is within the constellation Ursa Major. Getting back to Orion, each night as I look up at the sky, Orion's Belt seems to be in a slightly different position in the sky than it was the night or month before. That doesn't happen because it's moving but because *we* are!

A Moving Picture Show

Stars are fixed objects in the sky, just like our sun. The sun doesn't move or revolve around us like we used to think. We know now that the sun is fixed and we orbit around it. As we do, we are continually and constantly looking at different parts of space. This is what gives the stars and constellations the illusion of moving.

Think of it this way: Suppose you went to one of those giant outdoor malls built in a circular design, with a parking lot in the middle. Each shop has neon signs hanging in big windows at the front of the store. Now, stand in the middle of the parking lot and start rotating counterclockwise, from right to left. What happens? The stores appear to move from left to right, even though they are locked into a fixed position. It's an optical illusion. That's the same thing that happens with the earth and the stars and constellations in the sky. Try it sometime. Go outside and locate the North Star, Polaris. Look for a nearby constellation such as Orion. Lock its position in your mind. Go away for a few hours and come back. Orion will appear to have moved to the right relative to Polaris. This is because the earth is spinning in a counterclockwise motion on its axis. This is why the term *zodiac* has been used to describe the movement of the constellations, because it appears circular in nature.

Earlier we spoke about the power of pictures. We looked at how a short sequence of images can tell a larger story. I don't know about you, but I'm a visual learner. Reading something is one thing, but seeing it with your own eyes is something completely different. The ancient Hebrews, as well as other cultures, thought the same way. To illustrate this point, let's look at 1 Corinthians 1:22: "Jews demand signs and Greeks look for wisdom." Okay…what does that mean? The Greeks and the Jews had vastly different ways of expressing an attribute of God. For example, the Greeks would say that God is love. It's a short but accurate statement. It doesn't tell you how or why He loves you, just that He loves you. The Jews would say it this way: God is a shepherd. Phrasing it this way adds so much more to the character of God. How does a shepherd love the sheep? He protects them. He provides for them. He leads and feeds them. You see how using imagery to describe God can be so much more powerful than just using words?

God's desire is for all people everywhere to know Him. It's important to understand that initially, the message of the Messiah was confined to Judaism. It was the only religion in the world that had this concept. It was unique to the Jews. Christianity and the message of Christ spread to the rest of the world, but that was only after the resurrection of Jesus. That's why the disciple Peter had such a hard time going to the Gentiles. Up until that point, the Jews were the only ones who were looking. The Greeks, or Gentiles, mentioned in the 1 Corinthians passage were won to faith by reasoning, logic, and intelligent debate. The Jews needed a sign in order to believe.

We see this in the Gospels all the time. The Jews wanted more than just good preaching and nice sermons. They wanted a sign, and they needed one to convince them. That's why they were constantly asking Jesus for a sign. It was in their nature; it was their way. We can understand why God put signs in the heavens. It's why He calls the sun, the moon, and the stars "signs" over and over again. God knows His children. To the Gentiles He has given the Scriptures to convince us of the truth. To the Jews He has given the constellations, that they might also believe.

Looking for Zodiacs in All the Wrong Places

It seems that placing signs in the heavens, in the form of the zodiac, worked for the Jewish people. As I stated earlier in this book, I have been to Israel over forty times. I've been to every major city in Israel, from Tel Aviv to Jerusalem, from Haifa to Nazareth, and from Tiberias to Eilat. I have seen and experienced some pretty awesome things in the Bible Land. I've been privileged to participate in active archaeological digs and have been granted access to some very incredible artifacts and locations.

It was during a trip to Israel in August 2017 that I experienced one of my all-time highlights. I was able to visit a synagogue in the Jordan Valley in the region of the ancient city of Beit She'an, mentioned in 1 Samuel 31:12. There's a synagogue there from the sixth century during the Byzantine era known as Beit Alpha. I've had the privilege of visiting several ancient synagogues—many were far older than this one—but there was something that set this one apart from any other I had ever seen. The floor in the main meeting room had a mosaic floor containing all twelve signs of the zodiac.

Zodiac mosaic floor at Beit Alpha Synagogue

At first glance it seems very out of character for a Jewish synagogue to have a zodiac wheel in its main place of worship. It almost seems to be a direct violation of a prohibition given in the Ten Commandments in Exodus 20:4: "You shall not make for yourself an image in the form of anything in heaven above or on the earth beneath or in the waters below." It seems to be pretty cut-and-dried—no idols or images of any kind. God forbade the worship of them; He and He alone was to be worshipped.

So why did the builders of this synagogue commission such a contentious mosaic floor? It's a great

question. The answer is equally great, and it's found in
Genesis 1:14: "And God said, 'Let there be lights in the
vault of the sky to separate the day from the night, and
let them serve as signs to mark sacred times, and days
and years." Remember this? What purpose do the lights
in the vault of the sky serve? They serve as signs. To do
what? To mark days, months, and years. What does that
sound like? A calendar.

The Jews who built this synagogue weren't guilty of
idolatry or false idol worship; they were simply using
the very system that God had instituted for them at the
very beginning, at creation. There are other synagogues
around the world that also sport the signs of the zodiac.
Sadly, I'm unable to travel and see them all. But fortu-
nately for me, I don't have to go very far. Within a sixty-
minute drive from my house, in Toronto, there is a
synagogue that houses stained-glass windows with various signs of the zodiac on them. I was absolutely floored
when I first saw the Chabad Flamingo synagogue after I
was invited there to hear the firsthand story of a Holo-
caust survivor. That in and of itself was worth the journey,
but when I realized what was on the windows, I had to
ask the rabbi why. The building was only a few years old,
so the decision to include the zodiac in the design was a
recent and deliberate choice. He told me that the zodiac
served as a sign to them that God was indeed the creator

and designer of the universe! Incredible. Just as the Scriptures said two thousand years ago: Jews seek a sign.

Surely that must be a strictly Jewish practice. Certainly, no God-fearing church would ever include the twelve signs of the zodiac in its architectural design. But then there's the Chartres Cathedral in France. It was built in the twelfth century and is considered a World Heritage site by UNESCO. Its French Gothic design attracts visitors from all the world to gaze upon its spectacular beauty. There are many hidden treasures in this church, but the zodiac symbols on the stained-glass windows are not so hidden.

Constellation of Pisces depicted in a stained-glass window at the Chartres Cathedral

Why would a Christian church adorn its windows with the twelve constellations? Could it be that the earlier church knew something that we don't today? Perhaps they understood the meaning behind what Jesus said in Luke 21:25, that there would be signs, or constellations, in the heavens that would serve as the sign of the Son of Man. It's interesting to note that among the other images etched into the Gothic church's windows are scenes from the life of Jesus. Maybe they understood that God had marked the sky with celestial signs to confirm and affirm these very events from Jesus' life.

In many cases, as the old adage says, the church has thrown out the baby with the bathwater when it comes to the constellations. Yes, astrology is an ungodly practice that has hijacked the true purpose of the constellations, but if we allow it to remain hijacked, then there is the potential for millions, perhaps billions, of people to never hear or see God's story in the stars.

God went to extreme lengths to create, name, and align the stars in the heavens to form certain images that serve as a graphic representation of His plan of salvation. Just because the enemy and the world have sabotaged and marred the plan doesn't mean that we should surrender it so easily. I say that it's time the church reclaimed the wonder of the zodiac signs and returned them to their original purpose. I've already seen it happen as I have traveled around the world speaking on this very topic and have seen many unchurched people absolutely blown away by the connection of the constellations to the major activities in the life of Christ. It is powerful evidence not only for the existence of God as an Intelligent Designer but also for a God who loves and cares for His creation. Don't allow fear or past traditions to rob you of one of the greatest joys you'll ever experience.

Perfectly Perfect

Job 38 already told us that God is the one who both created and sustains the Mazzaroth. The precision with which the stars and planets align is on a level beyond human intelligence and understanding. The scale on which the universe is balanced speaks to the power of an almighty and loving God. Think of it: since the beginning of space and time, these constellations have been moving in their apparent zodiac paths, never deviating from their purpose. Night after night, month after month, year after year, they always do the same thing: they proclaim the glory of God and point us to His Son, Jesus. The chances of that happening on its own are incalculable. The chance of every major civilization in history depicting and preserving the exact same forty-eight constellations in the sky is also unimaginable.

We also have learned that out of the trillions and trillions of stars, only a small amount have been selected to serve the noble purpose of creating the outline for the constellations we see today. Further to this, we learn in Psalm 147:4 that "He determines the number of the stars and calls them each by name." The psalmist is telling us that God not only created the stars but also named them. That's a huge deal. That means the stars we see today that form the constellations weren't chosen or named by man. It's telling us that there is purpose in the decision, purpose in the choice. There are trillions of stars that are unknown and unnamed to us. How is it that the stars we do know of are the ones that form the constellation boundaries and outlines? Even though various cultures have different names for the stars and constellations in their own language, almost always they have the same meaning. It's far too much of a coincidence to be accidental.

Not only does God know all the stars that exist today, but He even keeps track of those that have disappeared. Isaiah 40:26 says, "Lift up your eyes and look to the heavens: Who created all these? He who brings out the starry host one by one and calls forth each of them by name. Because of his great power and mighty strength, not one of them is missing."

How can a star go missing? It's not like they can simply disappear. They don't. They go missing when they explode at the end of their life. They're called supernovas. They are majestic and mesmerizing to look at. The Hubble Space Telescope has given us incredibly sharp and detailed pictures of these celestial explosions. The colors of the gases and emissions from the star deaths are stunning. Even their deaths serve an important purpose as they aid in the formation process of new stars.

And the Winning Number Is...

We've been focusing on the nature and purpose of the constellations, but now it's time to take a detailed look at what they actually are and how they have been positioned to tell a story on a galactic scale. At first, the number of constellations may seem a bit confusing. You'll see figures such as forty-eight, twelve, and thirty-six. So how many are there actually? Well, the fact is that there are twelve, and thirty-six, and forty-eight.

Before I totally confuse you, let me explain why there are three numbers. In total, there are forty-eight constellations. This number is the sum of twelve and thirty-six. Twelve is the number of signs in the zodiac. Most people are familiar with this list: Virgo, Libra, Scorpio, Sagittarius, Capricorn, Aquarius, Pisces, Aries, Taurus, Gemini, Cancer, and Leo. Notice the order listed here is different than the traditional order associated with the astrological signs. That's because we are listing them in the order in which they reflect the life of Jesus. We begin with Virgo, which means "virgin," to represent the virgin birth of Jesus. This list ends with Leo because Leo represents Jesus as the Lion of Judah who will return as

All forty-eight original constellations

the conquering King. We'll look at all of these signs in greater detail in the upcoming pages. In the meantime, think of each of these first twelve signs as chapters. The next thirty-six signs will serve as chapter subheadings that further strengthen the meaning and story of the main sign. Each of the twelve signs has a subset of signs known as decans. These are called *decans* because when a circle of 360 degrees is divided by thirty-six signs, it equals ten, hence the prefix *deca*. So when we take the twelve main signs of the zodiac and add their thirty-six decans, we arrive at the number forty-eight.

All the ancient star maps show that these forty-eight constellations have been consistent throughout history. Two of the oldest star charts in existence come from

Zodiac of Dendera

civilizations that existed around five thousand years ago. The first, and most famous of the two, is known as the Zodiac of Dendera. This zodiac map was found on the ceiling of a chapel in an ancient Egyptian temple in the region of Dendera. Its remains are on display at the Louvre in Paris. It is very well preserved and has all forty-eight signs on it.

The second chart is an ancient Chinese zodiac, and guess what? It also shows forty-eight signs and constellations. In fact, dozens of ancient star charts have been discovered, spanning a wide variety of cultures and times, and they all show the exact same forty-eight constellations. Again, how is this possible, and how is it reasonable to believe that it is all one monumental fluke? Intelligent design seems to be the strongest answer.

Weird and Weirder

As we embark on this journey of discovery together, I feel like it's important to address an issue that is sure to come up as we study the images of the constellations. I'll be honest and just say it: some of them are pretty weird. No doubt that you'll agree with me as we start taking a closer look at each sign. Some of the signs make perfect sense; some of them, not so much.

Libra, a set of scales—that makes sense. Capricorn, half goat and half fish—not so much, right? Let me ask you a question. Do you believe that God uses imagery and symbolism to get a message across? I think the answer is yes. The Bible is replete with examples. Jesus once said that He was a door. He wasn't a door...but He was the door to the Father. He also said He was a vine. During the Last Supper He compared Himself to a loaf of bread. Are you starting to get the picture? (Pun intended.)

For me, the ultimate usage of bizarre imagery to convey a message is found in the story in Genesis 41. Joseph had been falsely accused of a crime, thrown in jail, and left to rot, but despite all that, he served God faithfully in his circumstance and God blessed him. One day the pharaoh of Egypt had a disturbing dream that, for the life of him, he could not figure out. The first stage of the dream involved seven cows emerging from the Nile River. They were fat and sleek and were grazing along the banks. So far, not too bizarre, right? Stage two of the dream involved some of the ugliest cows the pharaoh said he had ever seen in Egypt. Okay, now it's starting to get a bit weird. But here's the kicker: the seven ugly cows ate the seven fat cows. The pharaoh called on his magicians and wise men, who were at a total loss to understand the dream's meaning. No one could interpret such a crazy dream. As a last-ditch effort, the pharaoh called upon Joseph, and God instantly gave him the interpretation: God told Joseph that the seven fat cows represented a seven-year period of great abundance that was coming. The seven ugly cows represented a time of great famine that would follow the seven good years and completely eat up all the abundance from before. It made total sense! But until Joseph explained the imagery behind the dream, it seemed to be absolute nonsense and not important at all. It turned out that a dream involving handsome and ugly cows saved the nation of Egypt from total starvation and destruction.

I tell you all this so that you have a reminder when you get to some of the more out-of-the-ordinary signs in the zodiac. So let's dive into the constellations and discover the ancient message written in the heavens!

Can you draw? Are you a great artist? I wish I could say that I am, but the truth is, I don't have an artistic bone in my body. Thankfully, God, the Creator of the universe, is a master artist. Not only that, but He is also a master planner. When you first look at the forty-eight constellations on a star chart, or planisphere, the shapes and images appear to be random and kind of thrown together. But when you lay them all out and see everything all at once, clear patterns begin to emerge, and the more you look, the more you see.

Now, there are several ways in which we can proceed in our study of the constellations. While researching for this book, I laid out all the constellations on my office floor and had one of those "Eureka!" moments. I saw several distinct and complete sequences from the life of Jesus in the celestial layout. Just as God commanded generations before us to keep His legacy alive by telling stories to their children and their children's children, I now consider it my great honor and privilege to pass on this amazing legacy to you. Let's begin by asking a very simple yet very important question.

Why a Messiah?

According to the Scriptures, what was the Messiah's mission? What did He come to earth to do? Why did He need to come? What was so wrong with the human condition that warranted the need for a Savior? We know that it was promised that the Messiah would be born of a virgin. That He would be God in the flesh.

That He would be both fully man and God at the same time. That He would be crucified. The Bible specifically points to this kind of death when it says that He will be bruised and pierced and that we will look upon the one who was pierced. He was called the Lamb of God, who would be sacrificed for us as our Passover Lamb.

He would also serve as the scapegoat of Yom Kippur, as foreshadowed in the Book of Leviticus. It was promised that He would bear our sins and carry them away. That His perfect and atoning death would ward off the wrath of God as He paid the ultimate price for us by choosing to lay down His own life. No man could take His life, but He would willingly and lovingly lay it down for us. That His death on the cross would ultimately defeat the evil one and all his works.

It was promised that His resurrection would once and for all destroy the works of the devil. That He would set us free from the bondage and chains of the evil one. That He would rise from the dead. That He would ascend to the throne and be seated at the right hand of God as Supreme Ruler and King of Kings. If all of the heavens were made to declare Jesus, then *all* of this should be depicted in the stars and constellations.

Virgo

We begin with the constellation of Virgo. As we study the etymology of the name *Virgo,* a beautiful and powerful connection between this constellation and the birth of Jesus emerges. In virtually every known language, no matter what word they use, *Virgo* means "virgin." *Virgo* is derived from the Latin word *verginis*; the Greek word is *parthenos*. The Latin word means what you would expect it to—it refers to a woman who is a virgin. To understand the connection between this constellation, which refers to a virgin, and the miraculous virgin birth of Jesus, we need to look at the events of Genesis 3:15.

The first messianic prophecy in Scripture is given to us in Genesis 3:15: "And I will put enmity between you and the woman, and between your offspring and hers; he will crush your head, and you will strike his heel." At first glance, the text seems to be giving a fairly straight-forward message. It's a conversation between God, Adam, Eve, and the serpent. God takes a moment and speaks to each one, spelling out their punishment for their participation in the introduction of sin into the world. He'll deal with Adam in good time, but in this verse, God is dealing with the serpent. He's speaking about a time when the serpent's offspring and Eve's offspring will be locked into a battle of some kind. No time indication is given. We're just told that at some future date, this conflict will occur.

I don't know about you, but I find the phrasing of this story to be quite remarkable. God speaks specifically and only to Eve when mentioning her offspring. God doesn't say that the serpent's offspring will be in conflict with Adam and Eve. No, the statement is singular in nature and singles out Eve. How can this be? How can Eve's offspring reproduce without the participation of a man? Do you see the implication here? Somewhere down the line, one of Eve's descendants will produce an offspring without male intervention. It literally means that one day, a virgin will conceive and have a son who will defeat the enemy! Are you starting to get the picture?

We're all familiar with the Christmas story and the Bible verses used at that time of the year. With this new information, they are even more clear and powerful than before. Isaiah 7:14 tells us, "Therefore the Lord himself will give you a sign: The virgin will conceive and give birth to a son, and will call him Immanuel." It's basically a phrase-by-phrase reiteration of what God said back in Genesis 3:15. Who is it in the Isaiah passage that is giving the sign? God. Not a man or anyone else.

The idea of a virgin producing a child can seem illogical or even impossible to some people. How can this be? It's the same question Mary asked when the angel first told her that she would conceive. There's a process in nature known as parthenogenesis in which reproduction occurs without fertilization. If we break down the term *parthenogenesis* into its two root words, something very significant emerges. The first part of the word, *parthenos*, means "virgin," and the second part of the word, *genesis,* means "creation." So, when put together, *partheno-genesis* means that a virgin will create. This gives Isaiah 7:14 an even more vivid and powerful meaning.

Even the usage of the word *sign* in Isaiah 7:14 is significant. Remember how in Genesis 1:14 God said that the sun, the moon, and the stars would serve as signs? This is a direct fulfillment of that verse. The sign has a double meaning here—it's both natural and celestial—and it says that a woman, a virgin, will give birth to a son. Otherwise known as parthenogenesis! And the child will be called Immanuel—"God with us." The prophecy is that one day God will come to earth as a child so He can be with us, and that He will be born of a virgin. What an incredible thought. The God who created the heavens and the earth, who created space and time, wants to be with us.

Let's fast-forward from this prophecy to the time of Jesus. We all know it so well, don't we? But how much more will it mean now? The Gospel records tell us that Jesus was born of a virgin named Mary. She was engaged or betrothed to a righteous man named Joseph. He was furious when he found out that she was pregnant. What man wouldn't be? In his mind, there was no way this was possible. It took an angelic visit in a dream to convince him otherwise. And so it came to pass that the virgin gave birth to a son. Not only was it a fulfillment of Isaiah 7:14, but it was also a fulfillment of Genesis 3:15. As we look at the constellation of Virgo, we are reminded of God's extreme promise to intervene in human history and do what no man could ever do.

So that's the first important point about Virgo. The second is equally important. If you look at any star map with the constellation of Virgo, and I mean any star map, they may look slightly different in terms of facial features and clothing, but they all have one thing in common. In every depiction of Virgo, she is always holding a branch

Constellation of Virgo

in her hand. Big deal, right? That can't be as important as the virgin birth, but it is, because of what the Bible says it represents. Isaiah 11:1–2 says, "A shoot will come up from the stump of Jesse; from his roots a Branch will bear fruit. The Spirit of the LORD will rest on him—the Spirit of wisdom and of understanding, the Spirit of counsel and of might, the Spirit of the knowledge and fear of the LORD."

Holy smokes! Did you catch the prophecy in this verse? The Messiah will be the offspring of the line of Jesse, but here's the kicker: this messianic shoot from the stump of Jesse is referred to as the (capital B) Branch. What is Virgo holding in her hand? That's right, a branch! Let's put the two together. A virgin will conceive by the supernatural power of God. She will give birth to a child who will be called Immanuel, or "God with us." And the branch in her hands reaffirms the divinity of the child! But there's one more thing that has to do with the stars that form the outline of Virgo. Of all the stars in the constellation of Virgo, only a few names have survived over time. I'd venture to say that they were the ones that God wanted to outlast time. According to Richard Hinckley Allen's book *Star Names: Their Lore and Meaning*—the go-to guide on the origins and meanings of star names—in Virgo, there is a star named Zavijava, which also goes by its Arab name, Al Araf, which means "those who are sent forth." Another star, Porrima, goes by its ancient Roman names of Prorsa ("head first") and Postversa ("feet first"), the two positions in which a child can be born. Another is Vindamiatrix, known by its Arabic name of Al Muridin, meaning "those who are sent forth." *Auva*—also known as Lu Lim—means "gazelle, goat, or stag." Syrma, also known as Al Ghafr, means "he goat or king."

What's really interesting about Auva, though, is its position, right in the center of Virgo's womb. Since *Auva* means "goat," which is often interchanged with ram or lamb throughout the Scriptures, the child in the womb of Virgo was sent forth to be born as a Lamb and as a King. And as the Branch, He's also God. Boom!

While all ancient charts show Virgo holding a branch in one hand, some charts also show Virgo holding the scales of the constellation Libra in the other hand. The significance of this model is profound. If Virgo is giving birth to the miraculous messianic King who is divine, then He and He alone is the one who can balance the scales of Libra. As we will see in the discussion of Centaurus, Libra represents the imbalance of man's spiritual state and our need for One to come and bring that balance. Only a perfect sacrifice could literally tip the scales in our favor. I remind you again that the heavens exist to declare the glory of God, who is Jesus. He is the one who has the power and the ability to gain our redemption and pay the price for our sins. The sign of

Virgo set the stage and theme for the birth and purpose of the Messiah who was to come.

We've already gleaned incredible insight from Virgo about the nature and the birth of Jesus. Now we'll shift our focus to some of the constellations and their decans. They flow in the same vein as a comic strip or graphic novel sequence does. Some need only two constellations to tell a story, while others include between three and five signs to tell a more detailed story. But in every case, they depict an actual historical scene from the life of Jesus, or they play out an overarching theme of our Messiah's call during His life and ministry on earth.

Centaurus

As I pored for countless hours over the Zodiac of Dendera chart, which is over five thousand years old and therefore more accurately depicts the original alignment of the stars and planets, the first constellation that jumped out at me was Centaurus. At first glance, you may not see a spiritual story among the chaos of all the constellations surrounding it, but the story is there, and it comes straight out of several passages in the Gospels. As a reminder, think back to the pharaoh's dream about the skinny cows eating the fat cows. Bizarre, no doubt, but it came from God. In that same vein, the first constellation may also seem bizarre. Part man and part horse,

Constellations of Centaurus, Crux, and Lupus

we see that Centaurus has two natures in one. Other Christian writers throughout history have also picked up on the significance and symbolism of centaurs and have used them in books and stories. C. S. Lewis comes to mind with his Chronicles of Narnia series.

In this image, Centaurus is spearing the constellation of Lupus above a constellation called the Crux, also known as the Southern Cross. Just like ancient cave paintings tell a grand story by using only a few small images, in Centaurus, Lupus, and the Southern Cross, we see a picture of the sacrifice of Christ. He—who was both God and man—laid down His life and allowed

Himself to be pierced for us by being nailed to a cross. This is precisely what Jesus meant when speaking to a group of Pharisees. John 10:17–18 says, "The reason my Father loves me is that I lay down my life—only to take it up again. No one takes it from me, but I lay it down of my own accord. I have authority to lay it down and authority to take it up again. This command I received from my Father."

Jesus wasn't forced or coerced into giving up His life for us—He did it willingly. In fact, Hebrews 12:2 says we are "fixing our eyes on Jesus, the pioneer and perfecter of faith. For the joy set before him he endured the cross, scorning its shame, and sat down at the right hand of the throne of God." It was a joy for Him to lay down His life for us. He endured the cross because He knew it was the only way that we could be with God. He was the only one who was worthy and able to die in our place.

In fact, his substitutionary death on the cross was the only thing that could satisfy the justice of God. We were deserving of wrath and punishment, but His sacrifice turned it away from us. And wouldn't you know it, just under Centaurus and the Southern Cross lies the constellation of Ara. It's an altar of fire that it isn't turned toward them but away from them. His voluntary piercing and subsequent death on the cross turned the fire, the wrath of God, away from us!

Right above Centaurus is the constellation of Libra,

the majestic scales of heaven. They remind us that our lives hang in the balance and that the weight of our sins far outweighs our perceived righteousness. The Bible says in Daniel 5:27, "You have been weighed on the scales and found wanting." Nothing we could ever do could balance the weight of our sin. Only a perfect and spotless sacrifice could step in on our behalf and settle the debt. That happened when Jesus died for us and paid the price that we could never pay.

Just beyond Libra is the small but very significant constellation of Corona—the great crown of heaven. Only the King of Kings and Lord of Lords is worthy to wear such a crown. This makes the words of Hebrews 2:9 all that more impactful and meaningful: "But we do see Jesus, who was made lower than the angels for a little while, now crowned with glory and honor because he suffered death, so that by the grace of God he might taste death for everyone."

Christ's death for us is so clearly and beautifully pictured in this first group of constellations. But our journey is just beginning. There is much more to discover on our celestial journey. Let's go!

Sagittarius

The next group of constellations and decans involves Sagittarius and Scorpio, along with Ara again. In the previous set of constellations, we saw how the signs reminded us of Jesus' sacrificial death on the cross and how it paid the price for our sins as well as destroying the works of the evil one and disarming God's wrath. That is precisely what we see here again.

You might be asking: Why say the same thing again? There are a couple of reasons why that might be. First of all, repetition is one of the greatest teachers we have. Repetition is one of the greatest teachers that we have. No, the repeated statement is not a typo or an editorial oversight but rather an example of how repetition is a great teacher.

Second, it's always helpful to hear the same story from a slightly different perspective, or, as in the case of the Gospel writers, from as many eyewitnesses as possible. We see this happening over and over again with the synoptic Gospels. Often, something that Jesus did or said was recorded by different authors. The story is the same, but the details are slightly different. It doesn't make one account more accurate or better than another; the story is simply being told from each person's perspective. For example, Matthew was very much a Galilean Jew, and therefore his perspective of Jesus' life and miracles differed from the other Gospel accounts. He lived around the Sea of Galilee in the region of Tiberias, which was a very politically charged area. There were certain comments that Jesus could not make in that region. The Zealots, who were very religious and nationalistic, hated living under the tyranny of the Romans. They were waiting for the long-overdue Messiah, who was to come as a warrior king and lead them to freedom.

With that in mind, when Jesus performed miracles in that area, He told people not to tell anyone. Why? Because the Zealots might hear about it and want to crown him as king right there on the spot and lead a military campaign against the Romans. But when He was in other areas, He encouraged people to go and tell everyone what God had done for them. It's not schizophrenic or paranoid behavior. Jesus was just simply aware of His surroundings and acted accordingly.

Another example of the uniqueness of the various authors' perspectives is Luke, who was both a Gentile and a physician and saw things differently from other disciples. Even John, the beloved disciple, was in the inner circles of Jesus' ministry and was privy to conversations that some of the other disciples did not hear. The differences in their Gospels don't take away from the validity or accuracy of the accounts. In fact, the opposite is true. The diversity of perspectives adds honesty and authenticity to the Gospel narratives.

For the same reason, we will see repetition in constellations that tell the same story slightly differently. That's what happens here with Sagittarius, who has a bow in his hand. Like Centaurus, he's also a two-natured figure. The bow is pulled back and the arrow is ready to fly.

Constellations of Sagittarius and Scorpio

And like a cosmic picture book, the constellational chart shows us that the arrow is aimed directly at Scorpio, the great enemy. And once again, the altar of Ara and its fire are pointed away. As we saw in the first grouping, Jesus' actions cause the wrath of God to be taken away. Consider what the Bible says in 1 John 3:8b: "The reason the Son of God appeared was to destroy the devil's work." In this constellational setting we see Jesus achieving victory over the enemy on our behalf.

Before we continue, let's hit the pause button for a moment and reflect on what we just learned. Think about how these constellations just happened to line up to tell us about specific events and themes in the life and ministry of Jesus. These signs in the zodiac were there long before Jesus was ever born. There are those who believe that the universe has no design and that everything in it is just one massive and random accident. The early Christians didn't make up the shapes and images of the constellations after Jesus was born in order to make them look like they were speaking about or declaring Him. We know that they were already in existence, named and identified, for thousands of years before Christ ever came to earth. But how did the constellations survive over time? How is it that every major civilization throughout history has the same forty-eight symbols and signs of the zodiac? To say that it is random and coincidental doesn't add up and flies in the face of logic.

A Quick Babble about Babel

Whether Adam, Seth, or Enoch—or someone else for that matter—named the signs, the fact is that they have survived the test of time. We know from Jewish history that oral tradition was a very important part of that culture. That means that we can be fairly confident that whoever was the source of the names and images, they were passed down from generation to generation. Enter Genesis 11 and the Tower of Babel. From what we know from Scripture, everyone spoke the same language up to that point. After the Tower of Babel, God scattered the people around the world and gave those in each region their own language to speak from that point on. That means that wherever people ended up, they brought their knowledge with them, including astronomy. Although they remembered the shapes and patterns of the signs, a new name was assigned to the constellations because of the new language they now spoke. It's easy to see how different cultures evolved yet retained the same forty-eight images of the zodiac. Even though the signs were given new tribal names, their meanings have remained. That's why signs like Virgo mean "virgin" in every tribe and tongue.

I can't think of a single person in history who's come remotely close to being displayed in the forty-eight constellations. Think about that. These signs were in the sky and known by almost every ancient civilization in history. Long before Jesus was ever born, they knew He was coming. They didn't know His name, but they knew so much about Him. They knew His mission and understood what He was coming to accomplish.

His birth would be miraculous, and His death would be necessary. That's what we've seen in these first few constellations. But He didn't just come to be born and to die for us; He lived for us, too. His actions were a demonstration of how to live and how to treat others. Many great men and women have lived, but none of them had the universe designed to announce their arrival. That sends chills up my spine when I stop and really think about it. This next set of constellations demonstrate for us how He came to keep evil at bay.

Ophiuchus

One of the larger constellations of the zodiac is Ophiuchus. He's a tall and powerful figure. Remembering that the Jews seek a sign is key here. Imagine the ancients looking to the sky and recalling the story of Ophiuchus. The strong messianic overtones are undeniable and hard to miss. As you look at the other constellations right around him, a clear picture begins to unfold.

Ophiuchus preventing the serpent from reaching the crown

Directly involved with this sign are the constellations of Serpens, Corona, and Scorpio. Serpens is struggling to reach the constellation of Corona, which is a crown. But you can clearly see Ophiuchus is holding him back from ascending and taking the crown. What an incredible picture. If Ophiuchus is a picture of the Messiah, then we can see that Serpens is a picture of the enemy, Satan. He's called a deceiver and a snake many times in the Scriptures. But nowhere is it so clear as in the third chapter in the Book of Genesis. We briefly looked at this earlier. In the Garden of Eden, the serpent deceived Eve and caused sin to break into the world. The enemy's desire has always been to deceive mankind and to ascend above God.

The fact that Satan desired to rise up against God is stated emphatically throughout the Scriptures. It has always been his desire to sit in the seat of power and authority. He has always wanted to rule and reign and enslave mankind. He has lied, deceived, and twisted God's truth since the beginning of time. Locked into an eternal struggle with Almighty God, he is always and constantly trying to usurp God's throne and wear the crown as king. The clearest and most powerful illustration of this is captured for us in Isaiah 14:12–14: "How you have fallen from heaven, morning star, son of the dawn! You have been cast down to the earth, you who once laid low the nations! You said in your heart, 'I will ascend to the heavens; I will raise my throne above the stars of God; I will sit enthroned on the mount of assembly, on the utmost heights of Mount Zaphon. I will ascend above the tops of the clouds; I will make myself like the Most High.'"

Five times Satan declares his desire to overthrow God in this passage. Pay attention to these five "I will" statements he makes in these verses:

I will ascend to the heavens.
I will raise my throne above the stars.
I will sit enthroned.
I will ascend above.
I will make myself like the Most High.

Notice the direction he is trying to travel? Up. Always wanting to go up. He wants to ascend to the heavens, sit on a throne, and be like the Most High. Sounds like he wants to be king. And as you know, kings wear crowns. Now look at the constellations around Ophiuchus. Notice where Corona, the crown, is. It's up from where they are. What direction is the serpent trying to go in? Up. He's trying to ascend and become the king! Again, we clearly see that Ophiuchus is the one who is holding him back.

There's one more scene in the constellation of Ophiuchus that we have to talk about. We know that he has

Ophiuchus crushing the head of Scorpio

strong messianic overtones; we just saw that with the serpent. But located just below this massive figure is the constellation of Scorpio. Notice the positioning of these images. Let's remind ourselves that every major civilization that has produced a celestial sky chart shows it in the same way. Scorpio is always under Ophiuchus. The chances of all these star maps accidentally having these constellations in the same position seems highly unlikely.

You can see that the foot of Ophiuchus is in motion and moving toward the head of Scorpio—the enemy. It's also important to notice that the tail of Scorpio is in motion and is heading toward the heel of Ophiuchus. If that somehow sounds familiar, that's because it's a scene straight out of the Bible. It goes right back to what we spoke about in Virgo—that the offspring of the woman and the enemy would be locked into eternal conflict, until one day, the seed of the woman would crush the enemy. The prophecy was given in Genesis 3:15. This is another remarkable example of how God has arranged the constellations and put an incredible story in the stars. Really think about what is happening here.

The heavens were created to declare and point us toward the glory of God—Jesus. There's no stretching going on here. No leaps of faith are necessary to understand the story conveyed by this group of constellations. The picture is as clear as can be. Did the stars in these constellations just *happen* to be where they are? Did someone accidentally or coincidentally draw the lines that created the images that form these constellations? Out of the trillions and trillions of stars in the universe, did these just *happen* to be grouped together? A man holding a snake and preventing it from getting a crown is just a totally random cosmic collaboration? Honestly, I don't have enough faith to believe any of that. My eyes see what they see: Jesus the Messiah preventing the enemy from winning. There can only be one who wears the crown and can be called the King of Kings, and it's not Satan. It's Jesus. Period.

He wore two crowns. One was temporary and was for our sake, but the second is eternal and can only be worn by Him. During Jesus' trial, He was asked by Pontius Pilate if He was the King of the Jews. The Roman soldiers mocked him. They spat on Him and beat Him beyond recognition. They tried to further mock Him by making Him wear a crown of thorns and offering fake worship as they hailed Him as king of the Jews. They even hung a sign over His head as He was nailed to the cross that said "King of the Jews."

They were trying to shame Him. And in return, He prayed for them. The true King of the universe prayed for the ones who had just driven nails into His hands and feet. The King was not to remain dead. No. He would be elevated to the highest position in heaven; the resurrection made sure of that. Hebrews tells us that now He is crowned with glory. One day, all the world will know and recognize him as King. Listen to this epic and majestic description of Jesus in Philippians 2:6–11:

Who, being in very nature God, did not consider equality with God something to be used to his own advantage; rather, he made himself nothing by taking the very nature of a servant, being made in human likeness. And being found in appearance as a man, he humbled himself by becoming obedient to death—even death on a cross! Therefore God exalted him to the highest place and gave him the name that is above every name, that at the name of Jesus every knee should bow, in heaven and on earth and under the earth, and every tongue acknowledge that Jesus Christ is Lord, to the glory of God the Father.

Don't wait, make Him your King today! Revelation 19:16 says, "On his robe and on his thigh he has this name written: KING OF KINGS AND LORD OF LORDS." There may be trillions of stars in the universe, but there's only one star that matters: the Bright Morning Star, Jesus.

Boötes

Boötes is a constellation that doesn't get talked about very much these days, but that doesn't mean it's not important or significant. It's not one of the major twelve signs, but it is a decan of the constellation Virgo, along with Centaurus and Coma Berenices. In every sequence, each decan sets the tone of the story.

We took a pretty comprehensive look at Virgo at the beginning of this chapter, so I won't reiterate it here. What's important to remind you of is the promise that God made to Eve back in the Garden of Eden: that one day a virgin, one of her descendants, would conceive a child. That child would be God incarnate and die as the perfect sacrifice for mankind.

The decans of Virgo add a little more color to this picture. Centaurus, as noted earlier, is a two-natured figure representing God and man, together as one. In star maps that are five thousand years old and older, Coma Berenices is represented by a woman and male child. Again, this adds to and confirms what the main sign is saying—that the woman would bear a son. And finally, we have Boötes, the great herdsmen or shepherd with a sickle in his hand. This messianic figure with a sickle is referenced in the New Testament and points to Jesus.

Constellation of Boötes

So then, if Boötes is a messianic representation, then we should expect that his role in the zodiac would also be messianic in nature, and it is. Look at his placement in the zodiac. At first it doesn't seem all that strategic or relevant, until you start pulling in some of the nearby constellations and the story starts to take shape. Boötes' hand is holding a sickle that is in motion. He's not swinging it away from something but rather toward something. That something is the neck of the constellation Serpens. This is another representation of Satan trying to ascend above God by stealing the crown of Corona. Previously, it was Ophiuchus who was holding him back. This time it's Boötes, who is waiting to cut off his head if he tries to take the crown. Either way, the enemy will not succeed. Jesus the Messiah has it covered. I love what Psalm 68:21 says about this: "Surely God will crush the heads of his enemies." Repetition, the greatest teacher, is at work here again. God is reinforcing the idea that although the enemy will try and try to usurp Him, it will never happen because Jesus the Messiah has already defeated the enemy!

Orion

As we make our way through the constellations, I hope it's becoming evident that Jesus' life and mission is fully captured in the heavens. Sign after sign shows us the Messiah's power to overcome and subdue the enemy.

My mind keeps going back to Noah and his grandchildren sitting around a fire and looking up at the sky. It must have been a stunning sight, millions of bright stars against the black canopy of night. The figures and shapes of the constellations would have been much clearer and more discernible than they are today. There are very few places left on earth that can offer comparable skies.

In 2014, I was fortunate enough to visit a remote beach in eastern Australia and stare up at the night sky. I was almost moved to tears as the night sky put on a show for me that I will never forget as long as I live. I thought about the days of Abraham when God gave him the promise that his descendants would be as numerous as the stars in the sky. What a humbling moment that must have been for Abraham as he gazed at an almost infinite number of stars (Gen. 22:17).

The Belt of Orion, probably the most well-known and easily recognizable constellation, dominates the winter sky and can be used to locate several other stars and constellations around it. The three stars of Orion's Belt are Alnitak, Alnilam, and Mintaka. They go by many names in different cultures and have been associated with all sorts of imagery and figures, like the three magi. From our perspective, the stars seem to be perfectly lined up. That's the beauty of our position in the solar system. The apparent straight line of the stars in the Belt is possible because of where our solar system exists in the Milky Way, which is a spiral galaxy. The official term to describe it is "barred," meaning there are two main arms that make up the whole of the galaxy. We are located in what is known as the Orion Arm. Our solar system is perfectly positioned within our galaxy to allow us to see other stars and constellations.

As we look at Orion, there are a few striking features about him. Let's start with his name. The ancient Semitic language Akkadian, from as early as the thirtieth century BC, called Orion *Uru-anna*, meaning "heaven's light." *Or* means "light" in Hebrew, and many cultures refer to him as the "light bearer." The messianic

Constellation of Orion

connection with the constellation of Orion is striking. If Orion can be referred to as "heaven's light" or the "light of heaven," then Jesus' statements about being the light of the world are huge in their significance and connection to this constellation. The Gospel of John has the most references to Jesus as the Light of the World. In fact, the word *light* appears sixteen times in John, compared to only once in Luke's Gospel.

Jesus made several claims that shocked the people of His day. He made seven "I am" statements that definitely got the attention of his audience. They are recorded in the Gospel of John as follows:

"I am the bread of life." John 6:35
"I am the light of the world." John 8:12
"I am the gate." John 10:9
"I am the good shepherd." John 10:11
"I am the resurrection and the life." John 11:25
"I am the way and the truth and the life." John 14:6
"I am the true vine." John 15:1

All of these statements are powerful in their own right. However, since we are studying the constellation of Orion, the light bearer, let's take some time and consider Jesus' statement in John 8:12: "When Jesus spoke again to the people, he said, 'I am the light of the world. Whoever follows me will never walk in darkness, but will have the light of life.'" This is one of those statements that seem innocent enough on the surface, but Jesus, being a master teacher, knew how to say things in a way that took His audience on a journey—spiritually, emotionally, and academically.

His claim to be the light of the world was so contentious because of its connection to creation. As we look back to the first mention of light in the biblical narrative, we can begin to understand the power of this claim. It goes right back to Genesis 1:3–4: "And God said, 'Let there be light,' and there was light. God saw that the light was good, and he separated the light from the darkness." According to the creation account, in the very beginning, the world was dark. It was void and it was empty. It was without life.

Nothing can survive without light. Light is the source of all life. Once God introduced light into the world, the creation story began to unfold. Everything and anything that existed was because of the light that God brought.

One of the main prophecies and pictures of Orion is that a Messiah would come and bring down heaven's light, the source of all life. It would not only bring physical life but spiritual life as well. John 1:9 speaks of this: "The true light that gives light to everyone was coming into the world."

The ancients believed that Orion—a picture of the coming Messiah—would be the one to shine when things got dark. The Scriptures are replete with verses connecting Jesus to light and speaking of Him as the light of the world. We see it again in John 12:46: "I have come into the world as a light, so that no one who believes in me should stay in darkness." By claiming to be the light of the world, Jesus emphasizes that He was present at the very point of creation.

One final word about the constellation of Orion that serves as a great connecting point to the person of Jesus. Every ancient constellation draws him the same way, as a warrior with a shield. Now, the shield is consistent throughout history. It always has the same image on it, and that image is always a lion. It's very curious. Why a lion?

The Messiah is called many things in the Scripture. Some of His titles are the Lamb of God, the Bright Morning Star, Lord, the Branch, and the Lion of the Tribe of Judah, as in Revelation 5:5: "Then one of the elders said to me, 'Do not weep! See, the Lion of the tribe of Judah, the Root of David, has triumphed. He is able to open the scroll and its seven seals.'" This verse codifies everything that the previous constellations have been referring to. In Virgo we saw that a virgin would give birth to the Messiah, who would be called the Branch. The Messiah would come from the line of David; the Scriptures confirm that Jesus has a Davidic genealogy. And finally, the Messiah is referred to as the Lion of the Tribe of Judah.

Of all the images that could have been used for Orion's shield, the lion was chosen. Again, I ask, is it plausible that the selection of the lion was totally random and completely coincidental? Is it not a stronger possibility that God designed the constellations and placed this kingly insignia in the constellation of Orion? Over and over again, as the psalms have said, the stars are revealing knowledge night after night. They are screaming the story of salvation. Are we listening?

Taurus

Some constellations are more difficult to identify than others. For instance, if I asked you to point out Orion, you probably could—just find three stars on an angle to identify the Belt, and you've got Orion. Other constellations are either in the southern hemisphere, where we are unable to view them from North America, or they're so obscure and faint that they can hardly be made out with the naked eye. Not so with Taurus. Not only is it a huge constellation, but it also has some very obvious and recognizable features, namely the Pleiades and Hyades star clusters. The fact that these two star clusters "happen" to be positioned within Taurus plays an important role in understanding the story in the stars.

Constellation of Taurus

Aside from these two celestial markers, one of the most prominent and recognizable objects in the sky also falls within the borders of Taurus: the star Aldebaran. It's classified as an orange giant star. Aldebaran is over forty-four times larger than our own sun and lies approximately sixty-five light-years from Earth. I know that sixty-five doesn't seem like a large number, but remember what we said about Proxima Centauri at the very beginning of this book? It is only four light-years away and it would take us 137,000 years to get there, one way.

To give you a little perspective, on March 2, 1972, NASA launched the Pioneer 10 space probe. Eight months later, it arrived at Jupiter. It has since achieved what is called "space velocity," meaning it reached the minimum speed needed for an object to escape from the gravitational influence of a massive body, such as Jupiter. Pioneer 10 has left our solar system and is heading in the general direction of Aldebaran, and it should arrive there in about two million years or so. I hope they packed snacks.

If you follow the angle of Orion's Belt to the right, it will lead you straight to the orange giant. Just below it is the first star cluster, Hyades. The second, and more well known of the two, is Pleiades, which is off to the right, toward the outer center of Taurus. (Here's a quick interesting side note about Pleiades: although it is Latin in

Constellation of Pleiades

origin, the Japanese name for it is Subaru. Yes, just like the car.)

Taurus itself is positioned directly between Orion and Aries. As we've already seen, Orion is messianic in nature and Aries represents the Lamb who was sacrificed for the sins of humanity. Directly below Taurus is the constellation of Cetus, the great beast, who holds the constellation of Pisces in chains. Taurus is a bull always depicted in motion, as if he is charging toward something. He is. He's charging toward Cetus, the monster who enslaves. His front legs are raised, about to crush Cetus. Isn't that exactly what the other constellations were saying? That the Messiah was coming to crush and destroy the enemy and his works? Again we see the principle of repetition at work.

Imagine people in ancient times gazing up into the heavens and telling the story written in the stars to their children. You can almost feel the excitement of the children as their fathers tell the tale of the Messiah, the hero who would come down like a charging bull to trample the evil monster and set the people free. By the time they would get through all twelve signs, it was like they had just been watching a high-definition movie at an IMAX theater. Just as kids read about superheroes with special powers in comic books today, the images of the zodiac served the same purpose for the ancients in their day. I think that's pretty cool.

I'll Give You a Hint

Both Hyades and Pleiades have a connection to rain. *Pleiades* is from the Latin word *pluvial,* meaning "relating to or characterized by rainfall," and *Hyades* is from the ancient Greek word *hyein,* meaning "to rain." It's interesting that the two main features of Taurus are connected to water and that the constellation itself is a messianic picture of one in the heavens coming to trample and destroy the enemy.

One thing I've learned through my years of study in Israel about ancient Jewish culture is that it is very intentional. When Jesus used specific imagery in His sermons, it wasn't just filler—it was precise and intentional. For instance, when He called Himself the "Son of Man," it sounds like an innocent-enough statement to our modern ears. But to a first-century Jewish audience, it was blasphemy.

As a first-century Jewish rabbi, Jesus employed teaching methods that were unique to that time period. It was a style called *remez,* and it was known as a "hinting" method. You wouldn't come right out and say what you meant, but you would hint at it by making a statement that would cause your audience to know the portion of Scripture (in this case, the Tanakh, the text of the Old Testament) you were referring to and look it up.

When Jesus said He was the Son of Man, the audience

knew it was a direct allusion to a messianic reference in Daniel 7:13–14:

> In my vision at night I looked, and there before me was one like a son of man, coming with the clouds of heaven. He approached the Ancient of Days and was led into his presence. He was given authority, glory and sovereign power; all nations and peoples of every language worshiped him. His dominion is an everlasting dominion that will not pass away, and his kingdom is one that will never be destroyed.

Boy, does that language sound familiar. The Son of Man will be coming on the clouds with all power and dominion! It's the same language Jesus employed in Matthew 24. By making that one statement, Jesus caused His audience to recall this passage from Daniel and make the connection to who He said He was. The Gospel records are filled with this type of linguistic imagery.

Jesus also said that He was the bread of life. At first glance it seems like a nice spiritual allusion, but it goes much deeper, as do all the other illustrations He used. You see, He was born in Bethlehem, which in Hebrew means "house of bread." More than this, all the lambs that were to be used as Passover sacrifices had to be born in Bethlehem. You guessed it—precisely where He was born. (See my previous book *Understanding Jesus* for more cultural insights like this.) He was so intentional with every illustration and statement He chose to use. So when He refers to Himself as the living water from heaven, we should pay close attention.

Watercooler Talk

In Hebrew, words or statements can often carry a double meaning. This is one of those occasions. If Jesus truly is the living water that comes from heaven, then Taurus and its star clusters, whose names refer to water, serve as a very powerful messianic sign.

The word for *heaven* in Hebrew is an interesting one—*shamayim*. Because the Hebrew language is so complex and rich in imagery, many English words actually come from two or more Hebrew root words. This is the case here. *Shama* is an old Akkadian word that means "sky" while *mayim* means "water." The combined meaning of "sky water" helps us to better understand Genesis 1:6, which says, "Let there be a vault between the waters to separate water from water."

An ancient rabbinic belief is that the earth was encased in a liquid atmosphere at the beginning of creation, referred to as a canopy. There is much debate on the validity of such a theory. I mention it not to explain it but rather to remind us of the ancient belief that connected the idea of water existing in the heavens to something that Jesus claimed. When Jesus said He was the living water, He connected Himself to the idea that He left heaven to come down to earth and offer us this "living water."

A final thought on the messianic imagery found in the constellation of Taurus: it reminds us that there was a day when One came from heaven, like a charging bull, to trample the enemy who holds us in chains and has set us free. Another beautiful chapter from God's story in the stars.

Capricorn

It always amazes me how so much information can be gleaned from the simplest of pictures. Not only can you learn new things from pictures, but often, memories will also be attached to the photos. As I recently looked at photos from my wedding in 1990, I was amazed at the amount of memories that flooded my mind. If I closed my eyes and really thought about it, I could easily remember the excitement and anticipation of that day again. The same thing happens when I look at my children's baby pictures. I can remember the first moment I laid eyes on them and how I was immediately filled with such great love.

One of my most sincere desires in writing this book is that you would begin to feel the same way about the images of the constellations—that you would be amazed at the lengths God went to in order to tell you His story of salvation and redemption. That the meanings that the world and the enemy gave them would no longer come to your mind but that you would see them as God truly intended you to.

You may not see it at first, but the power and depth of God's love for us is all over the constellation of Capricorn. The imagery of this sign is so powerful. It's a beautiful reminder of the death and resurrection of Jesus.

Capricorn is one image made up of two distinct animals, a goat and a fish. I know how odd it can seem at first, but as we begin to break down the meaning behind the imagery, a beautiful picture unfolds. So what did the

Constellation of Capricorn

goat represent in ancient times? Sacrifices are mentioned all throughout the Scriptures, and two of the most prominent animals used, if not the most prominent, are the goat and ram. Genesis 15:9 is the first biblical reference to a goat and ram being used in a sacrificial ceremony. The next mention of a ram is in Genesis 22:13, where God provides a ram for Abraham to sacrifice in place of his son. This sets a precedent throughout the rest of the Old Testament. Over and over again, we see a lamb, a ram, or a goat being used as a sacrificial animal.

For me, the clearest messianic illustration is found in the ceremony of the two goats during the sacred day of Yom Kippur, also known as the Day of Atonement. The ceremony of the two goats of Yom Kippur is found in Leviticus 16:6–10:

Aaron is to offer the bull for his own sin offering to make atonement for himself and his household. Then he is to take the two goats and present them before the LORD at the entrance to the tent of meeting. He is to cast lots for the two goats—one lot for the LORD and the other for the scapegoat. Aaron shall bring the goat whose lot falls to the LORD and sacrifice it for a sin offering. But the goat chosen by lot as the scapegoat shall be presented alive before the LORD to be used for making atonement by sending it into the wilderness as a scapegoat.

Along with the two goats, notice that the first verse in this passage begins with the mention of a bull, which is the sign for Taurus. The story of sacrifice and salvation is continually interwoven through all of the signs. The high priest was to offer the bull as a sacrifice for the sins of his household and himself. Then he was to offer the first goat as a sin offering. The second goat was to be kept alive because of the very specific purpose it was to serve.

The priest was to lay his hands on the goat and symbolically transfer the sins of the people onto the goat, and it was to be released into the wilderness. The sacrificial goat bore upon himself the all the sins of the people. What a thought. That's exactly what Jesus did for us. He bore our sins. It's put this way in 1 Peter 2:24: " 'He himself bore our sins' in his body on the cross, so that we might die to sins and live for righteousness; 'by his wounds you have been healed.' "

How rich and precious is the imagery of the goat taking upon himself our sins and carrying them away? I'm so glad that the sacrifice of Jesus didn't just cover up our sins or take them away for another year but that His sacrifice was once and for all. This was the original intent of Yom Kippur—that the sins of the people would be carried away. However, it didn't always go as planned. Sometimes the goat would wander around and eventually make his way back to the camp. Can you imagine the shock and horror of the people? Their sins had returned!

To prevent this from ever happening again, the ceremony evolved over time. The priest would still lay his hands on the goat to transfer the sins of the people, but it was no longer released into the wilderness, for fear that it, and the sins of the people, might return.

A piece of scarlet wool was tied around one of the horns of the goat, and another was tied to a door in the temple in Jerusalem. The goat would then be taken to a high cliff where it was pushed off backward. The Jewish Talmud records that the scarlet wool would turn to white as the goat fell. When they saw this back at the temple, they knew their sins had been forgiven.

The basis for this tradition is said to come from Isaiah 1:18: " 'Come now, let us settle the matter,' says the LORD. 'Though your sins are like scarlet, they shall be as white as snow; though they are red as crimson, they shall be like wool.' " What a powerful picture. As the fulfillment of Isaiah 53, Jesus bore our sins, and because of His sacrifice, our sins have been made as white as snow.

Something Fishy

In the first half of Capricorn—the symbol of the goat— we see the death and sacrifice of Jesus. It would be a tragic and sad story if it ended there. But praise God that it doesn't. Just as the story of Jesus didn't end with the crucifixion, neither does the imagery of Capricorn. The goat transforms into a fish. Yup…a fish. I know what you're wondering: Why a fish? In many ancient cultures, the fish was a representation of life. At least seven other cultures have used the fish as a symbol for life. So how is this applied to the story of Jesus? What is the ultimate example of life in regard to Jesus? Without a doubt, it is the resurrection.

As early as the second century, Christians were already using the fish as a symbol for Jesus and for Christianity. It's a popular symbol to this very day. Also known as the ichthys, it's a Greek acronym derived from the statement "Jesus Christ Son of God and Savior." I'm sure you've seen it attached to a bumper of a car in front of you; maybe you have one. The point is what it represents. Jesus' crucifixion is at the heart of the Christian message—of that, there can be no doubt. But the message cannot, must not, and does not end there. The Bible states it clearly when it says in 1 Corinthians 15:14: "And if Christ has not been raised, our preaching is useless and so is your faith."

That's the beauty of the sign of Capricorn. The atoning work of Christ began with death on a cross, but it ended with life in the form of the resurrection! I can't imagine that it was the enemy who placed this message in the heavens, and I sure can't imagine that this sign created itself and just happened to picture so precisely the death and resurrection of Jesus. Can you?

Gemini

Gemini is one of those constellations that you may have heard of but know very little, if anything, about. Gemini is always depicted as a set of twins. Located not too far from Orion, the twins mark their place in the sky with two landmark stars: Castor and Pollux. Did you know that both of these stars, which each represent one twin, are mentioned by name in the New Testament? I'll show you that in a moment, but first we need to acknowledge the fact that we have missed many verses regarding astronomy, because we have confused it with astrology.

We've already seen in the Book of Job how some stars and constellations are mentioned by name. Jesus spoke of signs in the heavens marking the coming of the Son of Man. We're familiar with the Bright Morning Star of Revelation, but do we really understand what it all means and represents?

The apostle Paul was on a ship sailing to Rome. The Romans were very much into astrology and the worship of pagan gods. I find it interesting that the Bible records that the sign of Gemini was affixed to the boat that Paul was sailing on in Acts 28:11: "After three months we put out to sea in a ship that had wintered in the island—it was an Alexandrian ship with the figurehead of the twin gods Castor and Pollux." It just goes to show you that the signs of the zodiac were very much a part of

Constellation of Gemini

the world that the early church lived in. They were very much aware of its existence.

As I've stated before, I like to use the oldest star maps possible. Some of the newer ones have been changed and adapted to fit in more with modern times. So when I want to know what a constellation really looked like, I go back five thousand years. Ancient star maps by the Chinese and Egyptians show the twins to be males, but Gemini has been portrayed in various ways over the years. Some have the twins as female, and some have the twins only holding hands, with no objects of any kind. However, the further back in time we go, the more consistent the images are. Castor and Pollux are seen holding items, a harp and a weapon.

Why a harp and why a weapon? God chose to use these items because of the message He wanted to convey to the ancients. The two images of Gemini speak of the two appearances and purposes of the Messiah. One of the greatest challenges for some people concerning the messiahship of Jesus is that He is often accused of not fulfilling everything at His first coming. In order to dismiss Jesus as the Messiah, some rabbinic teaching states that He was supposed to fulfill all the prophecies at His first coming. This is a huge misunderstanding and cannot be found anywhere in Scripture.

One of the things I have learned about Judaism and the Hebrew language is that it is very poetic. It's not just rich with images and symbolism but also very beautiful in the way thoughts and words flow. There's a very well-known verse in Hosea that speaks to the two appearances of the Lord. It's often dismissed or overlooked, but when properly studied and explained, there is no doubt that it is speaking of two separate appearances. Hosea 6:3 says: "Let us acknowledge the LORD; let us press on to acknowledge him. As surely as the sun rises, he will appear; he will come to us like the winter rains, like the spring rains that water the earth."

Not sure if you caught what it was saying. The Lord will appear during the winter and spring rains. Those rains are at totally opposite ends of the calendar. Further to that, the rains in the spring are when all the feasts occur that Jesus fulfilled at His first coming. They include Passover, Unleavened Bread, Firstfruits, and Pentecost. The second set of feasts are to be fulfilled at His second coming, and—you guessed it—they occur during the winter rains. They include Trumpets, Atonement, and Tabernacles. So not only do the twins of Gemini represent the two appearances of the Messiah, but the objects in their hands speak to the nature and purpose of each appearance as well. In Gemini, the first twin is always depicted holding a harp. A harp represents peace, and it's also the instrument played by King David, from whom the messianic line is derived. The other twin holds a weapon, alluding to a more aggressive and violent second appearance. This may seem odd at first, but I assure you it's quite messianic in nature.

We have to go back to the life of Jesus to understand not only the two appearances but also their very distinct and different purposes. Much like today, the ancient Middle East saw its share of war. Many times, countries to the north and south of Israel would attack each other. If you look at a map of the region, you will notice that Israel is almost always at the center of the activity, usually not by choice. When two countries went to war, they would pass through Israel as the shortest route. You can imagine what a nightmare this situation created for the people of Jerusalem.

Imagine you are a person living in first-century Jerusalem. You go to the market as you usually do to get your fresh fruits and vegetables for the day. As you're leaving, off in the distance you see an army on the horizon. You freeze and ask yourself a very important question: Are they here to attack me, or are they just passing through on their way to another country?

So how would you be able to tell? And not just tell, but know instantly? Do you drop your groceries and run to sound the trumpet, or do you go about your business? A system was put in place to convey the army's intention to the people whose land they were traveling through. If they were on a mission of peace—they weren't there to attack, they were just there to refuel and rest before continuing on—the king or general would ride out ahead of the army on a donkey. This was a clear message and sign to the people that they were not there to attack you.

Can you now understand why Jesus rode a donkey down the Mount of Olives when entering through the Eastern Gate into Jerusalem? You see, His first coming was a mission of peace. He was here to reconcile people and God through His atoning death on the cross. This is what was referred to by the prophet in Zechariah 9:9: "Rejoice greatly, Daughter Zion! Shout, Daughter

Jerusalem! See, your king comes to you, righteous and victorious, lowly and riding on a donkey, on a colt, the foal of a donkey."

But what if the king was on a mission of war to attack? I'm sure you can imagine by now what animal he would ride out on ahead of the army: a horse. What does the Bible say Jesus will come riding at the second coming? A white horse, as seen in Revelation 19:11: "I saw heaven standing open and there before me was a white horse, whose rider is called Faithful and True. With justice he judges and wages war."

The sign of Gemini shows us that the Messiah makes two appearances, during the spring rains, or the spring feasts, and during the winter rains, the fall feasts. It also tells us that the Messiah's appearances differ in nature. The harp of Gemini not only speaks of the Messiah's mission of peace, but it even connects him to the house of David. The second symbol of Gemini, the weapon, speaks of the war and judgment that will accompany the Messiah at His second coming.

As we wait in hope of our Savior's return, we should be doing all that we can to tell those who do not yet know that they have a God in heaven who loves them beyond what they could ever understand or imagine. That He created a universe in which to display His incredible story of love. Hebrews 9:28 says it best: "So Christ was sacrificed once to take away the sins of many; and he will appear a second time, not to bear sin, but to bring salvation to those who are waiting for him." May we all do our part to point people toward Christ, and toward eternity.

Leo

Leo is known as king of all the constellations, and it is without a doubt my favorite. As we unpack its messianic meaning, you'll understand why it's the last out of the group of twelve signs. The lion traditionally symbolizes royalty and rulers. If Virgo is a powerful parallel of the Messiah's miraculous birth, then Leo serves as a picture of our Savior's triumphant return!

Constellation of Leo

Earlier, when looking at the constellation of Orion, we learned about the connection between the coming Messiah and the Lion of the Tribe of Judah. This is a powerful illustration, no matter what time period you are living in, but consider for a moment the implications it had for those living in antiquity. For us, the lion is a symbol of power, majesty, and strength, but to those living in biblical times, it was that and more. In order to understand why the symbol of the lion is so important, we first have to get a more ancient perspective before we can see it in a fresh, new, and exciting way.

As we remind ourselves of the purpose of creation—to point all mankind toward the Messiah—it shouldn't come as a surprise to anyone that the final sign of the zodiac is the crowning attestation to the Savior. Earlier we talked about how the concept of a Messiah was unique to the Jewish faith. It wasn't until after the resurrection that the Gentiles were grafted into the promise and invited to share in the blessing.

For thousands of years, even to this very day, the Jewish nation has been waiting and praying for the Messiah to come. The promise of the Redeemer was given in Genesis 3:15, but it's important to remind ourselves what that promise was: that there would come a day that the One would crush the enemy. The first glimpse of who this person might be is found in Genesis 49:8–10:

Judah, your brothers will praise you; your hand will be on the neck of your enemies; your father's sons will bow down to you. You are a lion's cub, Judah; you return from the prey, my son. Like a lion he crouches and lies down, like a lioness—who dares to rouse him? The scepter will not depart from Judah, nor the ruler's staff from between his feet, until he to whom it belongs shall come and the obedience of the nations shall be his.

The context of this passage is important. Jacob, whose name was later changed to Israel, was on his deathbed. His dying act was to put his house in order. With his twelve sons gathered around him, he began to speak, or prophesy, over them one by one. Then he got to Judah. The prophecy was not just for Judah in that moment but for his offspring as well. Jacob connects his son Judah to an image of a lion three separate times in this passage: he calls him a lion's cub, a lion, and a lioness on the hunt.

Each description of the lion paints for us a different aspect or character trait of the lion. The image of the cub is soft and playful, indicating the kind of relationship the Messiah will have with His own. To them He will be gentle. Next is a grown lion. Majestic, He protects and watches over His people. The final image is of the lioness on the hunt. Not only will the Messiah be kind and gentle, not only will He protect those under

His watch, but He will actively pursue anyone or any-thing that would seek to harm what is His. Here's the exciting part: *we* are His! That means that He is watch-ing over you, that He will never allow the enemy to come near you or bring you harm. This is precisely what God is demonstrating to us in this final sign of the zodiac. While some of the other signs are perhaps a little cryp-tic in their meaning, that's not the case with Leo. This lion is on the move and is ready to pounce. In fact, that's how we see this sign depicted in the most ancient of zodiac charts. His position in relation to the other signs is very intentional. Unlike some of the other signs that rely on nearby constellations to tell their story, Leo and its decans are uniquely positioned to tell a complete story. That's exactly what I would do if I were writing a story—I'd wrap it up nice and neat, with no loose ends.

Constellation of Leo and its decans: Corvus, Crater, and Hydra

The decans of Leo are Hydra, Crater, and Corvus. On both ancient and modern star charts, Leo is always either standing on the serpent (Hydra) or in a position of movement, ready to pounce on the enemy. The constellation of Crater is depicted as a bowl near the center of the serpent, and the constellation of Corvus, a raven, which is a bird of prey, is perched down near the end of the tail of the snake. Believe it or not, Leo and its decans are straight out of the Book of Revelation and are the perfect picture of what will happen at the end of days.

Virgo gave us the beginning of the story, and Leo brings the story to an epic conclusion. It makes total sense that Virgo finds its roots at the very beginning of the Bible in Genesis and that Leo, the last sign, finds its roots in the very last book of the Bible, the Book of Revelation.

We know that when the Messiah returns, He will come to make war against the evil one and totally destroy him and his works. We saw the two appearances of the Messiah pictured in Gemini. The first was a mission of peace, but the second will be different... *very* different. It says in Revelation 5:5: "See, the Lion of the tribe of Judah, the Root of David, has triumphed." He will triumph by defeating the evil one. The sign of Leo shows the lion seizing and trampling on the enemy, referenced in Revelation 20:2: "He seized the dragon, that ancient serpent, who is the devil, or Satan, and bound him for a thousand years."

The constellation of Crater represents the cup of God's wrath and fury, and it's depicted on its side, as if it's being poured out. See Revelation 14:10: "They, too, will drink the wine of God's fury, which has been poured full strength into the cup of his wrath. They will be tormented with burning sulfur in the presence of the holy angels and of the Lamb."

After the enemy is seized and trampled on, God's wrath is poured out on him. Look at what Scripture says will happen next in Revelation 19:17–18: "And I saw an angel standing in the sun, who cried in a loud voice to all the birds flying in midair, 'Come, gather together for the great supper of God, so that you may eat the flesh of kings, generals, and the mighty, of horses and their riders, and the flesh of all people, free and slave, great and small.'" The birds of the air will feast on the flesh of the defeated. This is pictured so clearly as we see Corvus positioned to feast on the flesh of the enemy, Hydra. There couldn't be a more appropriate ending to this story of the life, death, resurrection, and return of the Messiah!

One of the most rewarding things about being a believer is that we know how the story ends. Though we may pass through difficult seasons and circumstances, we have been assured that ultimately we will overcome and triumph. The Bible speaks to this in 2 Corinthians 4:17: "For our light and momentary troubles are achieving for us an eternal glory that far outweighs them all."

Everyone struggles in this life—Christian or atheist or anywhere in between. The difference is faith—faith in Jesus, that He will do what He said He would do.

God never starts something that He is not able to finish. Hebrews 12:2 says that Jesus is the author and finisher of our faith (KJV). I don't know where you are on your spiritual journey. Perhaps you've been on the journey all your life; perhaps you are not on the journey at all. No matter where you are, know this: you have a God in heaven who is for you and loves you beyond anything you could ever dream or imagine. He's not angry with you, He's not disappointed, He's not upset. He's like a loving father who is waiting for His son or daughter to return home. He drops everything when He sees you coming over the horizon and runs out to meet and embrace you. He's waiting for you. All you have to do is turn around and come home.

At the beginning of this chapter I laid out the mission and mandate of the Messiah. I also said that if the constellations were created to point us toward the Messiah, then His mission should be reflected in the zodiac. Let's take a quick look through the constellations to see if all His missions have been covered:

- Be born of a virgin
- Become God in the flesh
- Be crucified

- Be called the Lamb of God
- Be our scapegoat
- Carry our sins away
- Lay down His life willingly
- Pay the price through His death
- Destroy the works of the enemy
- Set us free
- Rise again

Without saying a single word, the heavens have been screaming the message of the Messiah and salvation to us. Are we listening?

The heavens declare the glory of God;
the skies proclaim the work of his hands.
Day after day they pour forth speech;
night after night they reveal knowledge.
They have no speech, they use no words;
no sound is heard from them.
Yet their voice goes out into all the earth,
their words to the ends of the world.
In the heavens God has pitched a tent for the sun.

(Psalm 19:1–4)

CHAPTER 4

JESUS WAS A VIRGO

A great sign appeared in heaven: a woman clothed with the sun, with the moon under her feet and a crown of twelve stars on her head.

—Revelation 12:1

Every great dream begins with a dreamer. Always remember, you have within you the strength, the patience, and the passion to reach for the stars to change the world.

—Author Unknown

ON FEBRUARY 6, 2018, SpaceX launched the Falcon Heavy rocket from the historic pad LC-39A at the Kennedy Space Center at Cape Canaveral in Florida. It's designed to fly to the moon and Mars, and thanks to the NASA Transition Authorization Act of 2017, we could see a human either on or near the surface of Mars by the early 2030s! Wow! What an incredible time to be alive!

My personal fascination with the stars began in 2013. It wasn't a rocket launch or rare celestial event that got me interested. It was a dream—an extraordinary and vivid picture that was painted for me one night as I slept, not an idea or a thought that I came up with on my own. Dreaming during sleep is a normal and natural occurrence for most people, but not for me. Sleep was a real problem for me between 2004 and 2016. During those twelve years I traveled around the world many times over speaking in churches and conferences. I crossed so many time zones each year that after a while, my body was no longer able to tell when I was in my own time zone, making it almost impossible for me to sleep.

For nearly ten years, the only way for me to get a few hours of sleep each night was by taking prescription sleep medication. The particular pill I was taking inhibited certain receptors in the brain that were responsible for dreaming. So basically, I hadn't had a dream in over ten years. You can imagine my surprise when I woke up one morning having had not just a dream, but an incredibly vivid one whose every detail I could remember. When I woke up that morning, my heart was racing. I could feel the adrenaline coursing through my body. I was buzzing with excitement as I began to recall the dream. To say it was bizarre would be a great understatement. Even now, I can remember what I saw as if it just happened last night.

I dreamed I was alone on an island in the middle of nowhere, lying on my back and looking up at the sky. It was very clear and very dark. Then, out of nowhere, the image of a woman appeared in the sky. She was young and she seemed very distressed. She wanted to run, but she couldn't move, as if her position was fixed in the sky.

Then a large, scaly, fire-breathing dragon appeared. It was angry and huge, and it wanted to harm the woman. I don't know how I knew that, I just did. But the dragon's position was also fixed and it couldn't reach her. There were other images in the sky also, and I couldn't make them out, but somehow I knew that they also had parts to play in the story. Then I woke up.

I felt like I had just watched a big-budget Hollywood blockbuster. The level of detail that I could see on the dragon was incredible. I lay there in my bed with my mind reeling, trying to make sense of what I had just seen in my dream. And then, as clear as anything, I sensed the voice of God speaking to me. I heard three words: "Check the constellations."

Zodiac Newb

You need to understand that at this point in my life, I had never studied or even looked at the constellations for any reason. Like most people, I had grown up knowing my so-called sign, but I certainly didn't pay any attention to it or know anything about it. I didn't even know how many signs there were. I didn't know what time of the year which constellation was out. Nothing. I literally knew nothing about them.

But... I knew that voice. I had heard it several times before in my life. It had guided me and helped me make some of the most important decisions in my life. The first time I saw Karen, the voice said, "She's your wife." That was it. Two years later we were married and I've never looked back. The voice told me to start my own TV show in Israel, I did, and it lasted for ten wonderful years. The voice told me to write my first book, and I did.

It had also helped me navigate through some difficult times in my life. So I knew it was the voice of God. But maybe this time it was wrong. Or maybe I hadn't heard it correctly. Because why would God tell me to check the constellations, the signs of the zodiac? The more I fought it, the more I knew I had to investigate. I began researching, but I wasn't getting any closer to discovering the meaning of my dream. And then it hit me: I had read about a woman and a dragon before. Not in some fantasy novel, but in the Bible. My heart began racing at the idea that this vivid dream I had had was in the Scriptures. And there it was. After a quick Bible search for the word *dragon*, the first reference I found was in Revelation 12:1–4:

A great sign appeared in heaven: a woman clothed with
the sun, with the moon under her feet and a crown of
twelve stars on her head. She was pregnant and cried
out in pain as she was about to give birth. Then another
sign appeared in heaven: an enormous red dragon
with seven heads and ten horns and seven crowns on its
heads. Its tail swept a third of the stars out of the sky and
flung them to the earth. The dragon stood in front of
the woman who was about to give birth, so that it might
devour her child the moment he was born.

I then learned that the word *dragon* appears four-
teen times in the Bible and all of the appearances are
in the Book of Revelation. Eight of them are found in
Revelation 12. I couldn't believe what I was reading. It
was exactly as I had seen it in my dream. I'm sure I had
read this verse at some point over the years, but I never
stopped to study it or give it a second thought. After all,
I had always been told that the Book of Revelation was
purely symbolic in nature. So I just resigned myself to
the fact that I would never be able to understand this
book and its many characters. Let's be honest, if the creatures and scenes depicted in the Book of Revelation are
in any way real, then we have a pretty scary future ahead
of us. Flying multiheaded creatures covered with eye-
balls. Let's just say it... it's a pretty weird and difficult-to-
comprehend book.

I must have read Revelation 12 a dozen times that day. I was desperately trying to make sense of this awesome scene of the woman and the dragon. What could it possibly represent? I read articles and Bible commentaries. I ended up being more confused than when I began. It seemed like everyone had a totally different interpretation of the images and story. Everyone was trying to spiritualize the imagery. Some said the woman represented the Church. Some said it was the nation of Israel, or possibly the Holy Spirit. Others said the dragon represented a brutal invading army that was coming; some said it was King Herod or the devil himself.

I wrestled with the many varying and conflicting interpretations. All I could do was to keep going back to those three words that I heard when I woke up—"Check the constellations." So I finally did. And I was truly shocked by what I found. If the woman in my dream really was a constellation, then how would I possibly be able to identify it? As I said earlier, I knew next to nothing about the constellations or the zodiac. I didn't know how many there were. I didn't know if the images were human, male or female, animals, or a combination of everything.

I quickly learned about the twelve main signs. To my surprise, there was only one female figure: Virgo. If the woman in my dream was truly a constellation, then the only sign she could represent was Virgo. My research led me to the Zodiac of Dendera. If Virgo was a constellation, then surely the dragon must be there also. And so it was—Draco, a massive and imposing constellation. And in the Zodiac of Dendera, Draco's mouth is facing toward Virgo, as if it wants to attack her. I nearly fell out of my chair when I saw it for the first time. Then it hit me. I mean, it really hit me. What if the woman and the dragon weren't symbolic? What if they were actual signs placed in the heavens to tell us a story?

Actual vs. Symbolic

In Revelation 12, John wasn't spiritualizing what he was seeing. He was describing the vision the Lord was showing him—not something happening in real time but something that had already occurred. In fact, the event depicted by the woman and the dragon was so important that God wanted John to preserve it for us. I read and reread Revelation 12. Then I went back to the beginning of the book to see if I had missed anything.

Most people believe the Book of Revelation was written about events that had not yet happened, that they were only prophetic in nature. But that's not necessarily the case, according to Revelation 1:19: "Write, therefore, what you have seen, what is now and what will take place later." Revelation seems to point toward three different time periods in this verse. Notice the details in the phrasing: "what you have seen, what is now and what will take place

139

later." Or, in other words, the past, the present, and the future. So, with that knowledge, what if in Revelation 12, John wasn't seeing an event that was going to take place. What if had already taken place? That changes everything we have come to understand about Revelation 12.

Think of the sky conditions in the time of John. Not only are we talking about the night sky two thousand years ago, but also John was on the island of Patmos in the middle of nowhere, where there was literally zero light pollution. The stars and constellations would have been brilliant and unobstructed. Nothing would have interrupted John's view of the sky or the horizon. He must have been absolutely blown away by what he was seeing.

A Celestial Calendar

The one historical event that that could possibly be the one described in Revelation 12 seems to be the birth of Jesus. So if John was seeing a vision of what the sky looked like on the night that Jesus was born, then understanding Virgo's and Draco's positions in the sky is crucial. By telling us that Virgo was in the sky, he's actually giving us coordinates from which we can extrapolate a calendar date. Remarkable! After all, the heavens exist to point us to Jesus. As we have already seen, celestial activity marked the crucifixion of Jesus. It's only logical that God would mark His birth also.

The two main signs that John tells about are Virgo

and Draco, but there's other activity that is extremely helpful in narrowing in on a specific window of time. John mentions specific locations of the moon, the sun, and a crown of twelve stars. He also mentions the sweeping of a third of the stars from heaven. It may all seem a bit overwhelming, even a tad confusing, but when we calculate all the locations of the celestial objects mentioned in Revelation 12, it all points to one magnificent date.

First of all, John mentions that the woman, Virgo, was clothed in the sun. This is a reference to the fact that the

Virgo clothed with the sun and the moon at her feet

sun was passing through the constellation of Virgo. This is quite normal, and in and of itself, it's not a spectacular happening. It gets more interesting with each item added to the picture. The next feature involves the moon being under her feet. Now we need to find a date on the calendar when the sun was passing through Virgo and the moon was passing under the feet of the constellation.

He also mentions that the woman had a crown of twelve stars. A group of twelve stars between Virgo and nearby Leo form a circular pattern above Virgo's head, something several star chart books refer to as the diadem, or crown, of Virgo. Today these stars are very difficult to see because of light pollution. But in John's time and at his location, they would have been so clear—clear enough to see with the naked eye. But John doesn't stop there. He gets even more detailed by mentioning the dragon's tail that sweeps a third of the stars out of the heavens.

A Dragon's Tail

This goes back to what we spoke about earlier when Jesus said, in Matthew 24, that the end times would be marked by stars falling out of the sky. As I mentioned before, what we think are shooting stars are merely space debris from comets or asteroids that penetrate our atmosphere. As they quickly heat up and cool down, it looks as if they

Constellation of Draco

are falling to earth. John is describing the same thing here by saying a dragon's tail will sweep the stars out of the sky. The dragon he is referring to is the constellation of Draco.

Every year we are treated to a massive meteor shower in the fall. The shower can happen as early as the second week of September and as late as the end of October. As the earth travels on its orbit around the sun, it encounters debris left behind by a comet. Thousands of particles slam into our atmosphere at extremely high velocities.

If you had never heard about a meteor shower or what caused them, it could certainly appear from your perspective as if the stars were falling from the sky. And because the meteors can emanate from the tail section of Draco, the dragon constellation, to John, it appeared as if the tail were sweeping stars out of the sky. Because this annual meteor shower takes place in the fall, the window for Jesus' birth becomes narrower and narrower.

Let's do a quick recap as we seek to understand what John saw that day in Revelation 12. The constellation of Virgo was in the sky as the sun was passing through it and as the moon was passing underneath the foot of the constellation. While rare, this has happened more than once. Add to this that the earth was passing through a meteor shower that emanated from the tail of the constellation of Draco at the same time that the sun and moon were crossing with Virgo. Now we have a much rarer occurrence. All these celestial events took place between September 10 and 12 in the year 3 BC. Leave it to the Creator of the universe not to stop there but to add even more celestial activity on the same day, to further verify the date of His Son's birth.

To establish a more specific date, we turn to what has been universally referred to as the star of Bethlehem. Just because it has been called that for two thousand years doesn't necessarily mean that it was a star. Don't get me wrong, there was a star involved. But there was so much more. It wasn't just a onetime, out-of-the-blue happening. There was a buildup to the day. So much so that it even caught the attention of nearby astronomers. You may know them as the Magi from the east.

Merry Christmas

The Christmas narrative is one of the most well-known stories in the world. Every year, on December 25, hundreds of millions of people around the world celebrate. Some people celebrate Christmas in honor of Christ's birth, some have no religious association with it and follow the Santa Claus tradition, and others simply view Christmas as an opportunity to connect with family and enjoy some time off. No matter why you celebrate, you've at the very least heard of the Christmas story and its connection to the birth of Jesus.

There are so many different decorations and recognizable items that are connected to this holiday. Everyone has either had or at least seen a Christmas tree. Christmas wreaths adorn front doors; there are lights on the roof and around the windows. Candy canes and gingerbread houses. After reading this, some of you are wishing it were Christmas right now! For all the Christmas traditions and items that exist, there are two that stand out above the rest and that will have our focus here. The first is the star of Bethlehem, and the second is the manger scene.

As a kid, you probably never questioned or even wondered what the star of Bethlehem was. Who cared, right? Christmas morning was coming, and that meant presents. But as we get older, we want to know and understand what we believe and why we believe it. I don't want to believe in something just because it has existed for a long time, especially if it's wrong or inaccurate. I want the truth. I want to know the truth. Because truth, and truth alone, is what sets us free. There have been a myriad of attempts to explain what the star of Bethlehem may have actually been.

What could have been so extraordinary that it would cause people from a faraway land to come and investigate? One idea that has been put forth is that it was a supernova, a star exploding at the end of its life cycle. The explosion is very bright and could last for days or even weeks. This would definitely garner the attention of astronomers. While it's a very good theory, there is no supernova on record during 3 BC.

Another working theory is that it could have been a comet traveling through our solar system. Again, that would explain the presence of a bright moving object in the sky that could last for days at a time. But we face the same problem: there is no comet on record for 3 BC.

Another, less likely scenario is what some refer to as a supernatural occurrence, that God created a star especially for the birth of Jesus. Is this possible? Of course it is. After all, we're talking about the God of creation here. But it doesn't seem to be in line with how God has worked in the past. The Scripture goes as far as to say that He never changes, that He is the same yesterday, today, and forevermore (Heb. 13:8).

What we often see in Scripture is that God uses the natural world that He created for His purposes. We see this in action during the ten plagues of Egypt. He used natural means to create a supernatural experience. God did the same thing with the parting of the Red Sea. He used wind and water to make a dry path for the people to walk through. So, while it's possible that God created a special star just for the night of Jesus' birth, biblical history pushes us toward the more likely conclusion that He used what was already there. Let's remind ourselves of what Matthew 2:1–2 says actually happened that evening: "After Jesus was born in Bethlehem in Judea, during the time of King Herod, Magi from the east came to Jerusalem and asked, 'Where is the one who has been born king of the Jews? We saw his star when it rose and have come to worship him.'" The star referred to in this passage was part of a series of celestial events over a period of several months.

The Not-So-Wise Men

Magi. Who and what were they? How many of them were there and where did they come from? The most important question is, *why* did they come? We'll get to that, but first, let's learn a little bit about these infamous travelers from the east and their role in history.

In English, we call them the Magi. This comes from the ancient Greek word *magos*. According to *Strong's Concordance*, the word is Greek number G3097 and is "the name given by the Babylonians (Chaldeans), Medes, Persians, and others, to the wise men, teachers, priests, physicians, astrologers, seers, interpreters of dreams, augers, soothsayers, sorcerers, etc." Given that this particular group of men were following a star, they were most likely astrologers, which, in ancient times, didn't mean what it means today. Astrologers then were people who observed and studied the movement of celestial objects. The better term, and the one I will use for them, is "astronomers" from the east.

I have a close friend in Israel who has served as my tour guide since 2004. His knowledge of the land and culture is staggering, and his wit and sarcasm regarding biblical characters is hilarious. I may call the Magi astronomers, but he humorously refers to them as the "not-so-wise men" from the east, because the Magi decided to tell King Herod of their mission to find the newborn King of the Jews. The danger of this statement is lost if you don't know the background behind the King Herod of the New Testament. During his reign as king, Herod grew increasingly violent and paranoid. He had his favorite wife, Mariamne, murdered on suspicion of conspiring against him. He also had several of his family members killed because he suspected they wanted usurp him. History records him as an absolute madman toward the end of his days. Enter the wise men, or the not-so-wise men. Herod, who has killed and murdered anyone in his way, now hears that a new King has been recently born. Without Herod's historical background, his actions in slaughtering all the boys two years of age and under in Bethlehem may seem extreme or shocking, but we understand that his actions were consistent with his narcissistic behavior throughout his entire reign.

As the title "Magi" implies, they came from the Arabian Peninsula, likely from either Persia or Babylon. The art of tracking celestial activity was quite common in these cultures, where they were very much aware of heavenly signs and their significance. The idea of astronomical activity and conjunctions with the birth or death of an important person was prevalent among these cultures. As we will see, the Magi were tracking a spatial phenomenon so intriguing that it caught their attention, and they risked the long and treacherous journey to Judea. Notice what they said to Herod in Matthew 2:2: that they had seen "his" star...not "a" star. That may not seem significant, but there was a huge difference.

Star Light, Star Bright

Some skeptics have discounted the "Bethlehem Star" story right from the get-go because of the fact that the Magi said they were following a star. Astronomically speaking, that's not entirely correct. If you recall from earlier in the book, we spoke about the fact that stars are fixed objects in space. They don't move, we do. So if that's the case, then how was it that the Magi were following a star? In order for them to follow it, the implication is that the star was in motion, so some have said that the accuracy and integrity of the passage is not to be trusted. Nonsense. They were following a moving object. They called it a star because at that time, they were unaware of the planets.

The word *planet* comes from the Greek *planetes*, which means "wanderer," and a planet is often referred to as a "wandering star." The ancients understood only two types of stars, fixed and moving, so when the Magi talked about following a star, they were absolutely correct in their description. The wandering star they were tracking in the sky was the planet Jupiter. That's right: the King Planet. It should come as no surprise to us that God would use Jupiter, the king of kings, to herald the birth of the real King of Kings, Jesus!

A Lion, a Planet, and a Star

Earlier in this chapter we listed the celestial activity of Revelation 12. We talked about the sun passing through Virgo, the moon at its feet, the crown of twelve stars, and the meteor shower emanating from Draco's tail from September 10 through the 12 in 3 BC. Remember those dates. They're about to become really important. We know from Revelation 12 that the constellations of Virgo and Draco were involved in the birth story. Now we will add one more: the constellation of Leo, the royal and kingly constellation. Again, it should come as no surprise that it is involved in marking the birth of the King of Kings.

Between September 10 and 12, a planetary movement called retrograde occurred. Retrograde is the apparent reverse motion of a planet on its course. This occurs because of the orbital position of the earth and the planet in retrograde. It actually looks like the planet is moving on its course as it normally does; then it slows down and eventually stops, then appears to go backward on its orbital course for a bit. It will look like it's slowing down and stopping again, and then it will reverse into its normal speed and direction. From our position on Earth, the retrograde path of the planet appears that it is moving in a circular motion and is sometimes referred to as a "halo" or "crowning" effect. Retrograde motion is not rare or unusual. In fact, Mercury goes into retrograde two or three times a year. So why would this retrograde capture the attention of the Magi? Because of the frequency of the retrograde and the fact that the planet was Jupiter.

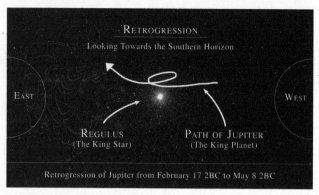

Jupiter's Retrograde of Regulus

The reason the Magi followed the Jupiter retrograde with such fervor is because not only did it rotate once or twice, but it also went into retrograde three times in an eight-month period. This is definitely not normal, as Jupiter usually only goes into retrograde once a year. Remember how we spoke about God taking what already existed and using it for supernatural purposes? This is a perfect example of that.

A planet can go into retrograde anywhere in our sky. It usually will perform its circle in open space, meaning it doesn't circle any particular star or constellation. It's still quite impressive to watch and observe. What made the retrograde of Jupiter so interesting to the Magi was not only that it did it three times but also that it didn't do it merely in open space. Jupiter circled, or crowned, one star and one star only. The star it crowned is called Regulus, and it's found in the constellation of Leo! But wait, it gets better. *Regulus* is Latin and means "little king."

Let's piece this all together. The King Planet, Jupiter, went into retrograde three times in eight months and crowned Regulus, the little king, in Leo, the constellation of the king. Are you starting to pick up on the "king" theme here? It's no wonder the Magi told Herod they had seen "his" star and asked where the King had been born.

They had never been to Judea. They most likely had never read the Hebrew Bible. But they were convinced that the heavens were revealing to them that a mighty King had been born. That's why they made the journey. That's why they risked it all. They knew that this was a once-in-a-lifetime occurrence. So the Bethlehem star was not just a star. It involved the star of Regulus, but it was so much more. It was an incredible combination of events—no wonder the Magi came from so far to see such an incredible event. They hit the celestial jackpot!

Remember the September 10 through 12, 3 BC, window we spoke of earlier? It's coming back again. The first time Jupiter went into retrograde and crowned Regulus was on September 11, 3 BC. I'm sure this sent the Magi packing. But then, only five months later, on February 17, 2 BC, it did it again! Jupiter crowned Regulus for a second time. I wonder if it was at that point that the Magi, with bags packed, decided to head for Israel. And

STORY IN THE STARS

three months after the second retrograde, it did it for a third time, on May 8, 2 BC.

I don't know about you, but there is *no* way that I could chalk this up to chance. This has intelligent design written all over it. This was intentional. This was on purpose, and it was *for* a purpose: to mark the birth of the most important person in the history of all mankind. The King Planet crowned the kingly star in the kingly constellation to mark the birth of the King of Kings. That's how our Creator God marked the birth of His Son! I don't know about you, but that is more than enough to convince me of a September 11, 3 BC, birth date for Jesus. But, as usual, there's more...

Sound the Trumpet

September 11 is a date marked by a more modern calendar than the one used in the time of the Bible. The twelve-month calendar we use today did not exist at the time of the Magi. So what calendar did they use? They used a biblical calendar that was centered around a lunar orbit. Our calendar is solar and runs for approximately 365 days, while the biblical calendar tracks the moon's orbit and runs for approximately 360 days. That's why Christian and Jewish holidays are seldom on the same day; our calendars are very different.

Since the ancient calendar uses the moon to track

and establish its days, it's no surprise that a new moon at the beginning of the first biblical month sets up the entire calendar year. The first month of the Hebrew calendar is called Tishri. Where our New Year occurs on January 1, the biblical calendar starts on Tishri 1, which generally falls on our calendar in mid- to late September. That's a very important date. Today, Tishri 1 is the Jewish New Year, but in ancient times, it was known as the first day of the Feast of Trumpets, called Yom Teruah in Hebrew.

When two witnesses confirmed the sighting of the new moon, it marked the beginning of the ancient Jewish calendar year. Then the rest of the year fell into place, and special ceremonies and joyous festivities took place that night. Yom Teruah translates into "Day of Trumpets" in English, in part because of what took place. Jewish tradition tells us that the ram's horn, known as a *shofar*, was to be blown one hundred times at the outset of Tishri 1. Can you imagine the sound? One hundred trumpet blasts resonating throughout the city.

Sounding the trumpet served various purposes. We're told in the Bible that the sounding of a trumpet can signal an alarm of war. It can also be a call to assemble the people, or even a command to march. It was also used to either announce or coronate a new king. We see an example of this in 1 Kings 1:34: "There have Zadok the priest and Nathan the prophet anoint him king over Israel. Blow the trumpet and shout, 'Long live King Solomon!'" In this biblical example, we see a connection being established between the blowing of trumpets and the coronation or installment of a new king.

September 11, 3 BC

You might be wondering why in the world I'm teaching Jewish history in a book that's supposed to be about the constellations. Here's why: Virgo was in the sky with the sun in her womb and the moon at her feet while wearing a crown of twelve stars on September 11, 3 BC. The dragon's tail went through a meteor shower from September 10 through the 12 and peaked on September 11, 3 BC. Jupiter, the King Planet, crowned Regulus, the little king, in Leo, the constellation of the king, on...wait for it...September 11, 3 BC.

September 11, 3 BC, was Tishri 1 on the Jewish biblical calendar and ushered in Yom Teruah, the Feast of Trumpets. The night that Jesus was born was Tishri 1. As the nation of Israel was celebrating the start of a new year and blowing the trumpet a hundred times, at a time that would be culturally appropriate to announce a new king—Jesus, the Son of God and the King of Kings, was born at that very time on that very night. That's how God announced the arrival of His Son!

The Beginning of the End

One final note about Revelation 12: Most people, myself included, only read verses 1–4 when speaking about the birth of Jesus being revealed in the constellations of Virgo and Draco. But the beautiful sequence of events that unfolded in order to show us His birth is only the beginning. The child in the manger is a beautiful and perfect moment, for sure. But His mission wasn't to make picture-perfect moments; His mission was to destroy the works of the enemy and set us free from the bondage of sin and death. We saw that repeatedly when we examined several of the constellations in the zodiac. We must keep reading Revelation 12 to discover what Jesus really came to accomplish and who He truly was. If all Jesus did was be born, that wouldn't have been enough.

Verse 6 of this chapter tells us that He will rule the nations with an iron scepter. This term should nudge our collective memory. We spoke of this as we examined what the constellation of Leo was showing us about the Messiah. Jacob called his sons and spoke a blessing and prophecy over his son Judah. In Genesis 49:10 he told his son that his descendants would rule like a lion one day, that Judah would be given a scepter to rule the nations, and that this scepter would stay in his line until the day the one "to whom it belongs" shall come. The scepter belongs to Christ and to Him alone.

Revelation 12:10 says that all authority, power, and salvation have been given to the one born of the woman in the vision: Jesus. The enemy is powerless against this Savior. The accuser of the brethren has been hurled down. Since the beginning of time it has been the enemy's desire to rule over humankind in the place of God. We saw it in the Garden of Eden, and we saw it in many of the constellations. But each time he has tried, he has been foiled.

The scepter and the right to rule belong to Jesus— the Lion of the Tribe of Judah. All of heaven and all of creation point toward Him as victor. This incredible story has been written in the stars since the moment of creation. Night after night, day after day, year after year, and millennia after millennia, the heavens have been pointing us to Jesus as the Way, the Truth, and the Life. I can't think of a single other person who has ever lived that even comes close to fulfilling the story in the stars. Can you?

Jesus is the King of Kings. That much has been made clear as we have studied the constellations. They told us of His coming and what He would do. They told us when He was born and what His mission would be. They told us of the incredible life that He would live for us. That He would come as a Lamb who would be sacrificed so that we might live. They told us that He would willingly lay down His life for you and me. That His death on the cross would pay the price for our sins.

You see, being born wasn't enough. Even dying for us wasn't enough. The only way He could demonstrate that He was truly divine and that He had power over sin and death was to defeat death. That's what we will look at in our final constellation in this study. Jesus said there would be signs in the sun, the moon, and the stars, and He told us to look to the clouds so that we would see the sign of the Son of Man. Be encouraged. No matter what you are going through, you have the victory, because He has already won it for you!

CHAPTER 5

THE BRIGHT MORNING STAR

I, Jesus, have sent my angel to give you this testimony for the churches. I am the Root and Offspring of David, and the bright Morning Star.

—Revelation 22:16

UP UNTIL THIS point, we have been dealing directly with the constellations themselves. Through them, we have seen the incredible way God orchestrated the greatest story ever told. Sign after sign pointed us to Jesus, who is the glory of God. The zodiac told us about the prophecy of His coming, about His miraculous virgin birth, His mission to destroy the enemy, and His sacrifice on the cross to pay the price of our sins and to set us free, and now, we will see how the resurrection and ascension have been depicted in the stars.

We've also made reference to one planet: Jupiter. This single planet gave us so much insight and understanding into some of the more prophetic and important aspects of the life of the Messiah. We first looked at Jupiter and its colossal impact from an incoming comet. As the king of all the planets, Jupiter painted a beautiful picture of sacrifice and love when it took the impact upon itself on our behalf. With its great velocity, that comet that was passing through our solar system could have been catastrophic had it hit the earth.

Not only was the comet's crash into Jupiter a beautiful demonstration of God's grand design and a stunning visual of God's protection, but it also showed us God's power and design over creation. Most recently, we looked at Jupiter and the role it played in the infamous "Star of Bethlehem" story. It captured the attention of the Magi with its celestial display of crowning the king star three times in eight months in the kingly constellation of Leo, and it led them across the desert to Bethlehem, to see the newborn King.

It's a Bird—It's a Plane—No, It's...

Each month, the night sky offers us a different show to watch. Looking up at the sky is like having the best cable package in the world. As we orbit around the sun on our journey of endless precision, we're treated to various stars, constellations, and planets throughout the year. Jupiter is a winter planet. For those who observe the night sky, looking at the great red spot on Jupiter is a fair exchange for having to put up with the cold and the snow.

Another celestial treat is the planet Saturn. Unless you know what to look for, you may mistake it as just another star in the sky. At first glance, and with the naked eye, it appears to be unremarkable at best. But with even an inexpensive telescope pointed at Saturn, you'll fall off your chair when you first see it. It's breathtaking!

I remember the first time I saw it with my six-inch Celestron telescope. I couldn't believe what I was seeing. The rings of Saturn were absolutely perfect—the planet was tilted in just the right way to give me an incredible view of them. They were almost too perfect. It was as if someone had printed out a NASA picture of Saturn and taped it to my lens without my knowledge.

Try it sometime; you will not be disappointed. I know that there are thousands of images of it online, but nothing compares to seeing it with your own eyes. This little speck of light in the sky is a planet that lies 746 million miles (1.2 billion kilometers) from Earth. It's amazing and humbling all at the same time.

I bet you've seen a star in the spring night sky that was so bright it caught your attention, and you were probably wondering which star it was. You couldn't help but notice it because of how bright it was compared to all the other stars around it. As soon as it gets a bit dark, boom... it pops. Well, the truth is, it's not a star at all. It's a planet: Venus. Our neighboring world, orbiting one step inward from Earth around the sun, is the third-brightest object in the sky, after the sun and the moon.

Meanwhile, Mars orbits the sun one step outward from us and is a very difficult planet to spot unless you know what you're looking for. It appears as a faint red dot in the night sky. Venus, on the other hand, is not a problem to spot at all. Not only is it the third-brightest object in the sky, but in the spring it is also by far the brightest of all the stars. In fact, next to the moon, it's the first object to shine at night. Why is it so bright? Some might think it's because of its proximity to Earth, but the truth is that its proximity doesn't factor into its brightness too much. After all, Mars is our neighbor, too, and it's very difficult to see. So why is Venus so much brighter than Mars?

Every planet collects and reflects sunlight at a different rate. When sunlight strikes a planet, some of the light is absorbed by the planet's surface or atmosphere, and some is reflected back out into space. The term used by astronomers to describe how bright a planet is *albedo*. Albedo is a comparison between how much light strikes an object and how much is reflected back into space. As you might have guessed, Venus has the highest albedo of any major planet in our solar system. So not only is it the first object to appear in the evening, but it's also the last to still be seen in the morning sky as the sun rises. Because of its ability to contend with the brightness of the sun, Venus has been called the "bright morning star." You might see where this is going. It's a classic example of how God uses the heavens to declare His glory. Let's take a brief look at our key text for this chapter, Revelation 22:16: "I, Jesus, have sent my angel to give you this testimony for the churches. I am the Root and the Offspring of David, and the bright Morning Star."

The first part of the verse is a throwback to an earlier prophecy in Isaiah 11 and was revealed in Virgo. It concerns the root of Jesse, which was a reference to the messianic Branch. The last part of the verse, which John says is a direct quote from Jesus, is about the Bright Morning Star. Not only is it a reference to the morning star, Venus, but also Jesus actually says the He *is* the Morning Star. That's a huge statement to make in light of what we have just learned about Venus.

Before we get too ahead of ourselves, let's remember what Jesus said concerning celestial signs in the heavens. In Luke 21:25, Jesus told us to look for signs in the sun, the moon, and the stars; that includes the morning star. Then in Matthew 24:30, He said the sign of the Son of Man would also appear in the sky. Now, add to that what Jesus just said in Revelation 22. Collectively, He's saying that the morning star is a sign in the heavens of the Son of Man.

Jesus is connecting himself as the Bright Morning Star to the planet Venus. I think the next logical question is *why*? Why call Himself the Morning Star, with the connection it has to Venus? I think that to answer that, we're better off letting Scripture speak for itself. This is what Jesus said in Revelation 22:13: "I am the Alpha and the Omega, the First and the Last, the Beginning and the End." I don't know about you, but I find His choice of words to be very interesting.

A few verses later He calls Himself the Morning Star, and here He says that He is the First and the Last. Remember what we said about Venus? It's the first star to be seen at night and the last star to be seen in the morning. It is literally the first and the last. So, if Jesus is making this connection to Venus, the astronomer in me wants to know where Venus was at key times in the life of Jesus. Was it in a significant part of the sky? Was it ever symbolically in any particular constellation during Jesus' birth, death, resurrection, or ascension?

I decided to use my astronomy software to run some sequences during key events in Jesus' life. To say I was shocked, surprised, and delighted would be putting it mildly. I decided to start with Jesus' birth on September 11, 3 BC. Guess what planet was in Virgo? Yup, Venus. There was one other planet in Virgo on that day also,

Mercury. Mercury has an interesting etymology and history.

In ancient times, Mercury was seen as a celestial messenger—he would deliver messages from the heavenly realm. *Webster's Revised Unabridged Dictionary* defines Mercury as a noun in this manner: "A carrier of tidings; a newsboy; a messenger." This is very curious language. Luke records that on the night of Jesus' birth, there appeared an angel in the heavens. Angels are messengers from God. This angel told the shepherds that he had good news, that he was bringing glad tidings to all the people. Isn't it interesting that on the night that Jesus was born, not only was Venus—the morning star—in Virgo, but Mercury—a celestial messenger—was also there to bring the message that the Messiah had just been born?

The idea of a person who brings information or is a celestial messenger already existed in the days of the apostles. There's a story that takes place in Acts 14. Paul and Barnabas were preaching in Lystra, present-day Turkey, when Paul noticed a paralyzed man in the crowd. They prayed for him and the man was instantly healed. Now, Barnabas was there in a support role. It was Paul who was the chief speaker, and he brought the message of God to the people.

The King James Bible preserves this story for us in a

most interesting manner. It uses two planets to describe Barnabas and Paul! See it for yourself here in Acts 14:12: "And they called Barnabas, Jupiter; and Paul, Mercurius, because he was the chief speaker" (KJV). Had you ever noticed this before? I hadn't. I was blown away when I first discovered this. The more I researched, the more and more sense it made to me why they used the two planets to refer to Barnabas and Paul in this manner. If people in antiquity really did use the name Mercury to refer to someone who brought a message from heaven, then you can understand why the King James Bible rendered it this way. Paul was Mercury to them because he was the one who did the speaking. The heavens really do declare the glory of God!

O Venus, Venus; Wherefore Art Thou, Venus?

The next main event in the life of Jesus had to be the crucifixion. Earlier we learned, based on very specific astronomical activity, that Jesus was crucified on April 3, AD 33, at 3 p.m. Logically, I set my astronomy software to show me the sky as it appeared in Jerusalem on said night. I have to tell you, the heavens did not disappoint.

I've been a Christian since the age of seventeen. I have celebrated many Christmases and Easter Sundays, and never in all my life have I ever been this excited to celebrate them now. There was a heavenly trifecta the day of Jesus' crucifixion. The three objects involved were Venus, the constellation of Pisces, and the sun. All of them fit the original description and purpose of Genesis 1:14, to serve as signs to mark significant times such as the holy days, which include the Feast of Passover—the same day Jesus, the Lamb of God, was sacrificed. Pisces was high in the sky that day. At 3 p.m. on April 3, AD 33, Venus was dead center in the constellation of Pisces. The sun was under the foot of Aries, as if being crushed, and Mercury makes another appearance here. Just as it was sent as a messenger to announce the birth of Jesus, it now sat just outside Pisces, declaring that the Lamb had indeed been sacrificed.

I don't know about you, but I'm thankful that the story of Jesus didn't end at the cross or in a borrowed tomb. Yes, He died for us, and yes, He paid the price for our sins, but more than this—so much more than this—He rose from the dead! Jesus not only spoke of having power and authority over sin and death, but by rising from the dead, He also demonstrated His power over sin and death.

On their own, fish have traditionally represented life or resurrection. In the case of Pisces, because the fish are chained and held captive by the great creature constellation of Cetus, they are symbolic of sin and death.

During the crucifixion, Venus—the morning star—was at its center. This shows us that the Bright Morning Star, Jesus, had been swallowed by death. The next sequence of events will show us that He didn't stay there, and neither did the morning star!

Up, Up, and Away

What would be the point of following Jesus if we could go to His tomb in Jerusalem and still see His remains? That wouldn't set him apart from any other religious leader that has ever lived. The Bible speaks of this in 1 Corinthians 15:14: "And if Christ has not been raised, our preaching is useless and so is your faith."

What's the one thing that sets Jesus apart? It has to be the resurrection. No other person in human history has ever claimed to have risen from the dead and ascended into heaven to sit at the right hand of God. No one. Absolutely no one. Christ, and Christ alone, has secured eternal life for you, because He Himself has it.

Eternal life and eternal youth have been at the center of many books and movies. In those stories, people have killed, lied, and stolen just to get close to eternal life. The story of Jesus' resurrection isn't some movie plot or action scene—it's reality. It's rooted in history. It had over two hundred eyewitnesses and disciples who testified to His resurrection until their dying breath.

They would never have given their lives for something they had concocted themselves and knew was an outright lie. They believed it to the point of death. That's the wonderful thing about following Christ—there's no death when it's over!

The heavens not only show us Jesus' birth and crucifixion, but they also tell of His resurrection and ascension to heaven. We know that Jesus was crucified at Passover as the Passover Lamb, that He rose from the dead, and that forty days later He ascended into heaven. As we have already seen several times before, this was also reflected in the constellations.

I feel it's important to stress again the point of the constellations. Everything that has been looked at in this book has been reflective in nature. We looked back and have seen how, time after time, God has used a celestial sign to mark an event in the life of Jesus. Although Gemini and Leo spoke of Christ's return, you'll notice that a date or time period was never given, nor did I try to find one. These constellations show us and confirm what the Bible says that Christ will do. That's all. Nothing more, nothing less.

Pisces shows us something beautiful about the mission of the Messiah: He came not only to destroy the works of the enemy but also to set us free from sin and death. And that's exactly what was pictured in the heavens from March 23 to May 6, AD 33.

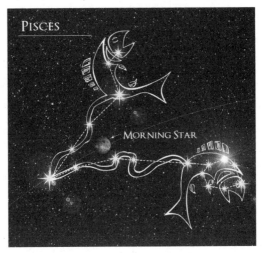

Venus in the constellation of Pisces

I tracked Venus' movement through the constellations for several months at a time, but it wasn't until I reached March 23, AD 33, that it started to get very interesting. That day, Venus entered the constellation of Pisces. Eleven days later, on April 3, it was dead in the center of Pisces. It continued on its normal trajectory until April 11. Then something happened. Venus went into retrograde. Instead of continuing to move in a straight line, it slowed down and gave the appearance of reversing course.

Curiously, the planet Mercury entered Pisces the same day that Venus went retrograde. Building on what we learned earlier about Mercury, it was about to witness and proclaim the most miraculous event in history.

Finally, on May 6, as Venus continued in its retrograde path, it broke through the chains that had been holding Pisces prisoner. That date coincided with the time of the ascension of Christ into heaven after defeating the enemy. After conquering sin and death, Venus, the bright morning star, broke the chains of bondage off of Pisces.

Was that not part of the Messiah's mission? Absolutely! Psalm 107:14 says: "He brought them out of darkness, the utter darkness, and broke away their chains." That's what Jesus came to do, and the heavens recorded it for all of time. No matter where in the world you live, no matter at what time in history you exist, the heavens are the same, and so is the story.

The prophet Isaiah spoke of it and Jesus later quoted from the Book of Isaiah when He stood in a synagogue in Nazareth before His peers. He stood to read the scroll that was apportioned for Him on that specific Sabbath, and God ordained for it to be Isaiah 61:1: "The Spirit of the Sovereign LORD is on me, because the LORD has anointed me to proclaim good news to the poor. He has sent me to bind up the brokenhearted, to proclaim freedom for the captives and release from darkness for the prisoners."

The sign of Pisces and the bright morning star are eternal celestial testimonies of Jesus' victory over death. Because Christ lives, so shall you. Be encouraged with this final thought from Romans 8:10–11: "But if Christ is in you, then even though your body is subject to death because of sin, the Spirit gives life because of righteousness. And if the Spirit of him who raised Jesus from the dead is living in you, he who raised Christ from the dead will also give life to your mortal bodies because of his Spirit who lives in you."

CHAPTER 6

LIGHTS IN THE SKY

The Sun of Righteousness will rise with healing in his wings.

—Malachi 4:2 (NLT)

AS FAR BACK as there has been recorded human history, humans have looked up to and worshipped the lights in the sky, namely, the sun and the moon. Archaeology in countries across the planet reveals this ancient attraction to celestial worship. Despite the Bible's strong warnings, mankind continued doing what they wanted to do. The early Roman Empire worshipped a sun god they named Mithra and even celebrated his birth from a rock on December 25.

The Aztec people worshipped a sun god named Tonatiuh, who they believed demanded a human sacrifice or else he would not move through the sky. The Tiv people from Africa considered the sun to be the son of a supreme being called Awondo, and the moon was his daughter. The most well known of those who worshipped the sun were the ancient Egyptians, who worshipped Ra as their sun god. But although many cultures worshipped the sun and moon as gods, many simply had a strong connection and infatuation with celestial objects and signs. We see their ruins to this very day.

One of the most famous ruins of a culture that observed the constellations is El Caracol, the observatory at Chichen Itza in Mexico. It dates back to the Maya civilization, where astronomers measured the movements of key objects in the sky. It's hard to believe how ancient it is because of how modern it looks. Yes, the building is dilapidated and clearly older, but the shape and dome design look like something that you would expect to see—and often do—in more contemporary observatories. The forward thinking of the Maya is amazing.

El Caracol Observatory

Stonehenge

Another famous ruin that has been shrouded in mystery is Stonehenge. Located in Wiltshire, England, it's one of the most enigmatic prehistoric landmarks. Theories of its origin abound: some say it was an ancient Celtic pagan temple; others say it's some kind of alien design. The monument's entrance faces the rising sun on the day of the summer solstice. For many, this suggests that ancient astronomers could have used Stonehenge as a solar calendar to track the movement of the sun and moon and mark the changing seasons.

This Is Not a Pyramid Scheme

While both of these ancient sites are spectacular and curious, there is one that trumps them all. Without a doubt, the most famous ancient structures linked to astronomy have to be the Pyramids of Giza in Egypt. I wonder how many movies show the pyramids. According

The Pyramids of Giza

to Wikipedia, there have been seventy-nine films shot in Egypt. I haven't watched them all, but I'm sure several of them have the pyramids.

The debate over who built the pyramids has been raging for centuries. Of course, you have your usual suspects and theories. Aliens make the top-five list for sure. Some have speculated that Hebrew slaves built them during the time of Moses. However, this is highly unlikely. As of 2008, an archaeological survey put the number of pyramids in Egypt between 118 and 138. Some of the oldest ones date back to 2630 BC, during the third dynasty. According to the available biblical data, the Exodus of the Israelites from slavery in Egypt occurred around 1450 BC. That leaves a gap of approximately 1,180 years between the earliest pyramids and the time of Moses. Given the fact there is more than a thousand-year discrepancy between the building of the first pyramids and the Exodus, any Hebrew slave involvement seems highly unlikely.

Whoever built them were geniuses of architecture. To think, these structures have lasted more than 4,600 years. I wish my house came with that kind of longevity! But for our purposes, the who and when are not what we are interested in. Our focus is on the why. Yes, the pyramids are amazing. They are massive and impressive and have stood the test of time. But why go to all that trouble? Other than looking really cool, what was the purpose in investing so much time, labor, and money?

We know that the pyramids served various purposes at different stages throughout time. Initially, they were built to serve as tombs. The higher the edifice goes, the more the steps decrease in size, until reaching an apex. It was said that the souls of the deceased would ascend the ever-narrowing steps until they reached the heavens. Astronomy is another possible usage for the pyramids, which contain a labyrinth of tunnels and hidden chambers that Egyptologists and archaeologists have been exploring for decades. Like most archaeological expeditions, these explorations sometimes raise more questions than they answer.

One question that arose was: Why do some chambers seem to be oriented toward specific places in the sky? One shaft in particular appears to be directly targeted at one of the stars in Orion's Belt. At first, it seems random and most likely by chance. As we have learned, the constellations are always changing positions in the sky because of Earth's orbit. So if it did align with a star in Orion's Belt, it would only be for a short period during the time when the constellation of Orion was in the sky. Curious.

Most Egyptologists suggest that Osiris is the Egyptian counterpart to Orion. They reach this conclusion because Osiris is the Egyptian god of resurrection and rebirth. So the shaft in the pharaoh's tomb that points toward Osiris/Orion is oriented this way in hopes that the pharaoh's spirit would either be regenerated or be able to travel between the realms of this life and the afterlife.

Aerial photo of the Pyramids of Giza

Further to this, the layout of the three pyramids does appear to emulate the three stars of Orion's Belt. Even the great historian Josephus appears to link the pyramids with ancient astronomy. We spoke of him earlier in connection to Seth and his descendants being the first generation of astronomers and cataloguing and observing the movements of the stars and constellations. We looked at the first part of verse 69, but here is the quotation in its entirety from *Antiquities of the Jews*, book 1, chapter 3, verses 69–71:

> They also were the inventors of that peculiar sort of wisdom, which is concerned with the heavenly bodies, and their order. And that their inventions might not be lost before they were sufficiently known, upon Adam's prediction that the world was to be destroyed at one time by the force of fire, and at another time by the violence and quantity of water, they made two pillars: the one of brick, the other of stone: they inscribed their discoveries on them both: that in case the pillar of brick should be destroyed by the flood, the pillar of stone might remain, and exhibit those discoveries to mankind: and also inform them that there was another pillar of brick erected by them. Now this remains in the land of Siriad to this day.

We need to remind ourselves of the incredible scrutiny that Josephus was under. The Romans were nothing if not

a well-organized military machine. Josephus was record-
ing not only the history of his people but also that of the
Roman Empire. Nothing would have been approved if the
powers that be were not satisfied with the absolute accuracy of his writings. That being said, there are two very
curious notes that Josephus makes in this passage.

Josephus claims that Seth's descendants were wor-
ried that their findings and research might one day be
lost. So in order to preserve their knowledge, he states,
they had all their information inscribed on pillars of
brick and stone. The term *pillar* was translated from the
Latin. However, Josephus' writings were originally in
Greek. The word he used was *pyramus*, from which we
get our modern word *pyramid*. Interesting.

So Josephus makes a connection in his writings
between the earliest human knowledge of astronomy
to the pyramids. Further to this, according to Josephus,
the ruins of these pyramids were in the land of Siriad,
that is, Egypt. If this in fact is the case, and we don't have
any reason or evidence to doubt Josephus' accuracy,
then a passage from Isaiah becomes very, very interesting: "In that day there will be an altar to the LORD in the
heart of Egypt, and a monument to the LORD at its bor-
der. It will be a sign and witness to the LORD Almighty
in the land of Egypt. When they cry out to the LORD
because of their oppressors, he will send them a savior
and defender, and he will rescue them" (Isa. 19:19–20).

The Egyptians added one more monument that seems to connect with astronomy. We know it as the Great Sphinx of Giza, a bizarre creature with the body of a lion and the head of a woman. Some say the connection between the lion and Leo is unavoidable and mirrors the position of Orion's Belt and the constellation of Leo in the sky, while others suggest that the Sphinx sets the proper order of the constellation. Starting with the face of a woman, it's possible that it represents the only female sign, Virgo, and it ends with a lion, which can only be Leo. If that is true, then the proper order of the zodiac would be to begin with Virgo and end with Leo. This is precisely what we have seen in the constellations and their alignments and connection to the life of Jesus, from His virgin birth to His triumphant return as the Lion of the Tribe of Judah.

Where Do We Belong?

Why do I tell you about the Maya, about Stonehenge and the pyramids? I'm not trying to prove any ancient or mythical connection to astronomy. I'm not even saying that these theories and interpretations are 100 percent correct. No, I do it to show you how desperately humankind has wrestled with the purpose of our place in the cosmos. Think of the billions of dollars that have been spent in that pursuit. Consider the centuries of labor, planning, and construction of these massive and monumental ancient astronomical devices. They were hoping, even believing, that their connection to the universe through false gods would somehow give their lives meaning; trying to use ancient methods to deduce and foretell what their fates would be; developing entire disciplines of study to determine what the heavens might be telling them. For all their struggles and efforts, I can't help but think of what the prophet Isaiah said: "All the counsel you have received has only worn you out! Let your astrologers come forward, those stargazers who make predictions month by month, let them save you from what is coming upon you" (Isa. 47:13).

God does speak to us through the heavens. We have seen this time and time again through the various constellations. We don't need to invent gods or go to extreme lengths to understand what He has purposed to say to us through His creation. If we will simply listen and observe, the message will be clear and our hearts will be full. After all, the heavens have been declaring God's glory since the beginning of time. Unlike those before us who attempted to deify the sun and the moon and to make the stars say something they never intended to say, let's learn some lessons from creation. We've learned about life, love, and eternity from the Son of God—now let's learn a thing or two about the sun of

God. As the Scripture says in Psalm 113:3: "From the rising of the sun to the place where it sets, the name of the LORD is to be praised." I wholeheartedly agree!

I've been blessed to serve the Lord in some pretty exciting and amazing opportunities. I've traveled around, teaching and speaking in churches and at Christian events. I've met some great people along the way and have fond memories that will last me a lifetime. From 2002 to 2016, I traveled to Israel on a regular basis. Sometimes I would lead Christian tours, other times I would go to write new material and visit friends. But mainly, I went to film segments for my TV show, which I hosted and produced for ten years.

I crawled through two-thousand-year-old tombs filled with human remains. I lay in a sarcophagus that was filled to the brim with Crusader-period skulls and bones. I made wine by stomping the grapes with my own feet, just as the ancients did. I even learned how to make a tea similar to something that Abraham would have drunk.

For all the amazing adventures that I went on, perhaps my favorite thing to do in all of Israel was to get up before the sunrise, grab my cameraman, and film a time lapse. We've captured the sunrise over the Red Sea in Eilat, the Sea of Galilee, the desert fortress of Masada, and over the Temple Mount and the Mount of

Olives in Jerusalem. Breathtaking. I'll never forget those moments.

Sun vs. Son

As I drove around Israel on those early mornings, I began to notice something that I had taken for granted virtually all my life. And when you hear what it is, you'll likely identify with it also. Have you ever been driving somewhere early in the morning, and you notice that the sky is just starting to turn from the black of darkness to a slightly brighter shade? My personal favorite moment is when the sky starts to burn red or orange, with streaks of bright white. Before you realize it, the sky has gone from total darkness to light in just a matter of a few minutes.

But here's the interesting thing to me: the sun isn't even up yet, but you can see its effects before you see it. When you see the light, you know that the sun will soon follow. I find that fascinating. The astronomical term for this is *twilight*. Simply defined, twilight refers to the illumination of the lower atmosphere when the sun is not directly visible because it is still below the horizon. So even though you can't directly see the sun, you know it's coming, because its light goes ahead of it.

I know what you're thinking. This isn't new information. You've probably seen this twilight phenomenon dozens, if not hundreds, of times as you drive to work. I have, too. But all of a sudden, it was different. One day, it just made more sense to me than it ever had before. To be honest, a lot of what I have written in this book is not new. You've probably noticed that there haven't been a lot of sources cited in this work. It's not for a lack of research. If I'm being honest, I don't think I've ever researched so much for any other single project I have ever done. Much of the information I have presented here is public knowledge. Here's the difference: I just simply made the connections.

It's public knowledge that on September 11, 3 BC, the sun, the moon, Venus, and Mercury were in Virgo and a meteor shower in the Draco constellation occurred. I can't find a source for that anywhere. It hasn't been written about before. But I can run the dates and sequences in my astronomy software and watch it happen. What I've done that is different is connect the day of Jesus' birth to John's vision in Revelation 12.

The same goes for all the constellations that I have already mentioned. I can't, and don't have to, find a source to tell me when the constellations were in the sky. They just were. It's really that simple. That's what I'm doing with the sun. I'm drawing on naturally occurring parallels from creation and making the connection to the historical person of Jesus of Nazareth.

Just as we see evidence of the sun of God before we

actually see the sun, we were also given evidence about the Son of God long before we ever saw Him. The evidence came in the form of biblical or messianic prophecies. In fact, did you know that there are over three hundred prophecies in the Old Testament that tell us about the coming Messiah? We were told who He would be. We were told where He would be born, what He was coming to do, and even why He had to come at all. Just like the sun, long before we ever saw Him, we saw His light. It's a powerful principle that we see at work in creation.

Another truth we know is this: nothing can stop the sun from rising. It can be cloudy. It can be raining. It can be snowing. It could be summer. It could be winter. You could be having a great day, you could be having a bad day. It doesn't matter what you do or say, the sun is coming. They say that you can be sure of two things in this life: death and taxes. Sadly, this is true. But I'd like to propose that we add a third item to that guarantee: the sunrise. No matter what is happening in the universe, the sun will rise over the horizon. Even though we see its light before it rises, nothing can compare or challenge the power of the light once the sun is in the sky. The higher it rises, the more light it gives off. The more light we have, the better we can see and the more life thrives on our planet. It's the same principle with the Messiah.

The Light of the World

Just as nothing could stop the sun from rising, the same was true of Jesus. No matter what Israel went through or what it did, nothing could have prevented the Messiah from rising. Jesus truly was the Light of the World. How many times do we see that in the New Testament? Jesus said He was the Light of the World, and then He proved it by healing a blind man. Just as the effect of the sun increases as it rises, so it was with Jesus, who said in John 12:32: "And I, when I am lifted up from the earth, will draw all people to myself."

Sometimes we take the presence of the sun for granted. When you wake up in the morning, you just assume that it will be there, emitting its life-giving light. When you draw back the curtains after you get out of bed, you anticipate the warmth of the sun's rays on your face. Like most things in this life, we don't know how much something means to us until it's gone.

Life could not exist on earth if were not for the sun. We could still survive if most things were taken away, but not the sun. Light is necessary for almost everything we do. What's the first thing we do when the power goes out? We either get a flashlight or light a candle.

Just as God's word is a lamp that lights our path, the Messiah's life lights our hearts and spirits. There is a beautiful prophecy in Isaiah 9:2 about the power of the coming Messiah's light: "The people walking in darkness have seen a great light; on those living in the land of deep darkness a light has dawned." The prophet Malachi also tells of the Messiah's light in Malachi 4:2: "But for you who fear my name, the Sun of Righteousness will rise with healing in his wings" (NLT).

I love the illustrations that we can extract from nature, specifically the sun. We don't have to stretch or imply; the truth and the life lessons are right there on the surface, waiting to be discovered.

Have you ever wondered about the varying climates and temperatures on earth? After all, aren't we all exposed to the same sun? So how is it that it can be freezing in one part of the world yet blistering hot in another place? The answer can be long and convoluted. But the simple answer can be boiled down to one word: position. Our position on earth determines the amount of direct sunlight we receive from the sun and its strength. Because of the equator's relatively flat angle to the sun, it receives the maximum amount of direct sunlight. As we move north of the equator, the earth's angle increases and the land receives less direct sunlight, energy, and heat.

What a powerful parallel for us! We have to position ourselves to receive God's Son into our lives. We must take up a posture of surrender and humility if we want to receive God's power in our lives. Just as the equator is at the center of the earth and receives maximum exposure to the sun's power, we too must keep the Son at the center of our lives so that we can experience Him and His power fully. James agreed with this principle and states in chapter 4, verse 8: "Come near to God and he will come near to you."

I was attending a service at my home church recently when my friend and pastor Daniel Clarke was speaking. As usual, it was an excellent message. But for me, the best part of the message wasn't theological in nature. It was when he shared a story of his dear nana, his grandmother, who had passed away several years earlier.

Her name was Nita Morris and she suffered from polymyositis, an uncommon inflammatory disease that causes muscle weakness on both sides of the body. She suffered great discomfort, especially toward the end of her life. When she passed, Daniel was given his dear nana's Bible. She had slept with it under her pillow each night. It's what got her through some dark and difficult times.

She never, ever gave up on God. In fact, on the very last page of her Bible was a handwritten note that she had jotted down through her weakness: "I believe in the sun, even when it's not shining." Wow! She could say that in the midst of her suffering; what about you? What about me?

You see, she believed in the very principle I mentioned above. Nothing can stop the sun from rising or shining. Clouds may get in the way and temporarily block the sun from our eyes, but it's there; it's always there. The same is true for us today. You may find yourself in a dark place today. Perhaps it was something that you did, or maybe it was something that was done to you. The principle is the same. You may not see the sun shining right now, but whatever is blocking the light, it will not last forever. It will pass, and the sun will shine and fill you with its life-giving power.

Over the Moon

So the sun is the first light in the sky that was spoken of in Genesis 1:14. The other light was the moon. As with the sun, we have seen how God has used the moon throughout history to mark His story. We see how He has ordained for full moons to be in the sky during holy days like Passover and Tabernacles. He has also used lunar eclipses as signs in the heavens to mark sacred days and important times in the life of Jesus. He also uses them as a tool to teach us how to live for Him each day.

Have you ever gazed up into the night sky on a clear night and looked at the moon? I mean, *really* looked at the moon? I've looked at it through binoculars and telescopes. I've felt like I almost lost my eyesight on a few occasions. I would see bright spots for several minutes after. How is that possible? How can the moon blind me with its light, considering the fact that it has no light source of its own? Have you ever thought about that? There's something really awesome that we can learn from this.

Earth has a very robust atmosphere that is critical to sustaining and protecting life. The moon also has an atmosphere, but it is infinitesimal compared to ours. This thin atmosphere is what allows the sunlight to reach its surface. The moon shines because its surface reflects light from the sun. The key thought here is that the moon has no ability whatsoever to generate light; it simply and only reflects the light it has received from the sun. And despite how bright the moon seems to shine at times, it only reflects between 3 and 12 percent of the sunlight that hits it.

Isn't that the truth with us, too? There's no light in us. The Bible says that there is not a single righteous person on earth. All we can do is reflect the *Son*. I love how this is stated in 2 Corinthians 3:18: "So all of us who have had that veil removed can see and reflect the glory of the Lord. And the Lord—who is the Spirit—makes us more and more like him as we are changed into his glorious image" (NLT).

What else can we learn from our lunar companion? Consider what it takes in order for a lunar eclipse to occur. We talked about this at an earlier point in this book. The science behind it is quite simple. A lunar eclipse occurs when the earth comes between the moon and the sun. This prevents the moon from receiving any direct sunlight, thus sending it into eclipse mode.

How many times do we go through a personal eclipse? Think about it this way. Every time we allow something in this life to get between us and the Son, we go into eclipse mode. What sorts of things do we allow to block out the direct light of the Son in our lives? Sometimes we allow sin to interfere with God's presence. Sometime we allow doubt, worry, anxiety, and all kinds of other issues to block our time in the presence of God.

I know it's easier said than done, but we need to learn to trust that God has it covered. Remember, we serve the God of creation! There's nothing that happens to us that He can't help us through. Sometimes we eclipse ourselves by allowing things to get in the way. Sometimes it's the actions of others that cause us to go into eclipse. In all things, we need to learn how to totally rely on and trust in God. Jesus said it best when He spoke these words two thousand years ago in Matthew 11:28: "Come to me, all you who are weary and carry heavy burdens, and I will give you rest." Cast all your burdens at the feet of the Son today and learn to rest in Him.

What's the most important relationship in your life? Perhaps it's with a spouse or a child. Maybe a best friend

or coworker. I would venture to say that the most important and enjoyable relationship you could ever experience is with God, through His Son, Jesus. Just as it's so
important to invest in the relationship with a person in
your life by spending time with him or her, so it is with
God. The more time we spend with Him, in His presence, the more we will reflect His glory and the more
people will see Him in us.

It's the same with the moon's relationship with the
sun. The moon goes through various phases. We've all
seen it. Whether it's a new, half-, or full moon, we all have
seen it at different phases in its cycle. What causes the
moon to change its appearance? Again, the answer can
be boiled down to one thing: position. The more direct
sunlight it receives, the more it shines. The less sunlight
it receives, the less light we see being reflected from the
moon, causing its different phases.

By now I'm sure that you can see the obvious parallels between the moon's relation with the sun and our
relationship with the Son. The more time we spend in
God's presence, the more people will see His light and
love reflected in us. Because of its position to the sun,

Moon phases

sometimes you can barely see the moon at all. If and when we allow things of this world to get in the way, it becomes difficult for people to see God's light or love in us. So what can we learn from all this? Don't allow anything or anyone to hinder your relationship with the Son. Soak it in, reflect it, and let others see the love of God living and shining in you!

CONCLUSION

I STARTED OFF by stating that tens of thousands of words have been written about the first ten words of the Bible. Consider these forty-six thousand or so words to be my contribution to bringing more understanding to this very important topic. Writing this book has been a labor of love.

For a long time now, I have passionately believed that God has placed a story in the stars. From that night I dreamed about the constellations until this very moment, this message has been burning within my heart, and I have longed to share it with the world. Moving forward, my prayer for you is that your relationship with God will never be the same again. That your awe, love, and respect for Him has increased exponentially. And, if you have not had a relationship with Him, that the information in this book would compel you to start living in relationship with God.

If you're a believer, I hope this book has helped you to think. If you're a thinker, I hope this book has helped you to believe. Don't just believe my words; believe the evidence. Follow it to its natural conclusion. I believe that if you follow the path to God that has been set forth in this book, you will find Him.

I have one final exhortation to leave with you. If all of creation exists to declare God's glory, and if the glory of God is Jesus, then I urge you to listen to creation. Hear the voice of heaven today. Investigate the knowledge that has been left for us.

I challenge you with this one last thing. On the next clear night—wherever in the world you live—get a star chart, stand outside, and look at the placement of the constellations in the sky. Don't just take my word for it—see the story in the stars with your eyes. And once you see the story, share the story, so that others may also experience the extravagant, the extreme, and the eternal love of God!

> *The heavens declare the glory of God;*
> *the skies proclaim the work of his hands.*
> *Day after day they pour forth speech;*
> *night after night they reveal knowledge.*
> *They have no speech, they use no words;*
> *no sound is heard from them.*
> *Yet their voice goes out into all the earth,*
> *their words to the ends of the world.*
>
> —Psalm 19:1–4

The Word became flesh and made his dwelling among us. We have seen his glory, the glory of the one and only Son, who came from the Father, full of grace and truth.

—John 1:14

*Praise the L*ORD.
*Praise the L*ORD *from the heavens;*
praise him in the heights above.
Praise him, all his angels;
praise him, all his heavenly hosts.
Praise him, sun and moon;
praise him, all you shining stars.
Praise him, you highest heavens
and you waters above the skies.

—Psalm 148:1–4

ACKNOWLEDGMENTS

This book would never have happened had it not been for divine intervention. God showed me the story in the stars in a dream. It would be several years before I could write about it, but the seed was planted in one single night. I'm still not sure why He chose to reveal it to me, but I'm so glad He did.

On December 8, 1990, I stood by the love of my life and exchanged vows. We promised to love and support one another through the good and through the bad. Even in the darkest of times, she has been my light. She has encouraged me every step of the way. I'm both proud and amazed at how this book has turned out. That would not be the case if it had not been for her. She poured countless hours into editing and refining this manuscript. She has helped me in more ways than you could ever imagine. Karen: I love you! Thanks for riding this crazy journey with me!

I'm proud of many things I have accomplished in my short time on this earth, but nothing I have ever done compares with the joy that our two children have brought us. Katelyn and Daniel have encouraged me every step of the way. They made me laugh when I needed it. They spoke words of life into my soul when it felt like it was dying. I love you two crazy kids. You da best. And I love that God gifted us with one more child: Aaron. I'm so glad that God brought you and Katelyn together. Thanks for laughing at my "dad jokes" and for always being a source of encouragement.

FaithWords has believed in me from the very beginning. From my first book to this one, Rolf Zettersten saw something in me and took a chance on this unknown Canadian. Words are not enough to express how thankful I am for you. Thanks for believing in me.

Several people helped this dream become a reality. Hannah Phillips is one of those people. A good editor listens to the voice of the author when reading a manuscript. Hannah, thank you for allowing me to be myself in this book and for allowing me to have a conversation with my readers and not a boring lecture. You made hundreds of adjustments that I never would have been able to make on my own. Thank you for making me a better writer. I would also like to thank Kallie Shimek and Erin Granville for all their patience and thoughtfulness in their additional editing.

Where would anyone be without their mother? Mom, I'm so thankful that you and Dad sacrificed so much so that I could have the incredible opportunity to live in this country and pursue my dreams. I love you, Mom! Dad, I miss you every day. You're always in my heart. You're gone but not forgotten.

My in-laws, Clyde and Marion Williamson, have been such an incredible blessing to me. They've treated me like a son since day one and have never stopped praying for me. I appreciate and love you both so much.

Thank you, Sophia Cabral, for almost losing your mind by reading the manuscript nonstop in such a short period of time. Your comments and wisdom made me a better writer. Paul and Sophia, I'll never forget the day we all went to the Kennedy Space Center and had our minds blown together. You guys are awesome, and we're so thankful that God had our kids marry one another!

Real friends stick with you through thick and thin. They believe in you and encourage you when you need it. Brian and Jessica Mayes are those kinds of friends. I told Brian about *Story in the Stars* long before it ever materialized. He spoke such life into my vision and helped me to believe that I had been given something special. You guys are awesome and I love you both. P.S. Canada Dry is made in Canada!

All through my teenage years and my early Christian life, there was one band that ministered to me over and over again. That band was Stryper. Never in my wildest dreams did I ever think that we would become friends.

They took me in and welcomed me into the amazing Stryper family. To Michael Sweet, I say a huge thank-you. He believed in *Story in the Stars* from the very beginning. I remember his reaction from the very first time he heard the vision. He used his platform to spread the vision all across the nation. Michael and Lisa, thank you for the awesome journey of this friendship. I love you both...Honestly!

Some friends you've had for a long time, and then some friends you've just met but their impact on your life is incalculable. That's who Jim Warner Wallace is. When I needed guidance, God brought him into my life at just the right time. You're a good friend, even though you're from California! ☺

Thank you, all of you who have played a role in my life and helped me become the man I am today.

APPENDIX A

1. Andromeda
2. Aquarius
3. Aquila
4. Ara
5. Argo
6. Aries
7. Auriga
8. The Band
9. Boötes
10. Cancer
11. Canis Major
12. Canis Minor
13. Capricorn
14. Cassiopeia
15. Centaurus
16. Cepheus

17. Cetus
18. Coma
19. Corona
20. Corvus
21. Crater
22. Cygnus
23. Delphinus
24. Draco
25. Eridanus
26. Gemini
27. Hercules
28. Hydra
29. Leo
30. Lepus
31. Libra
32. Lupus
33. Lyra
34. Ophiuchus
35. Orion
36. Pegasus
37. Perseus
38. Pisces
39. Piscis Austrinus
40. Sagitta
41. Sagittarius
42. Scorpio
43. Serpens

44. The Southern Cross
45. Taurus
46. Ursa Major
47. Ursa Minor
48. Virgo

APPENDIX B

1. Virgo
    a. Coma
    b. Centaurus
    c. Boötes

2. Libra
    a. The Southern Cross
    b. Lupus
    c. Corona

3. Scorpio
    a. Serpens
    b. Ophiuchus
    c. Hercules

4. Sagittarius
    a. Lyra
    b. Ara
    c. Draco

5. Capricorn
    a. Sagitta
    b. Aquila
    c. Delphinus

6. Aquarius
    a. Piscis Austrinus
    b. Pegasus
    c. Cygnus

7. Pisces
    a. The Band
    b. Andromeda
    c. Cepheus

8. Aries
    a. Cassiopeia
    b. Cetus
    c. Perseus

9. Taurus
    a. Orion
    b. Eridanus
    c. Auriga

10. Gemini
    a. Lepus
    b. Canis Major
    c. Canis Minor

11. Cancer
   a. Ursa Minor
   b. Ursa Major
   c. Argo

12. Leo
   a. Hydra
   b. Crater
   c. Corvus

ABOUT THE AUTHOR

JOE AMARAL has traveled the world many times over as a sought-after Bible teacher, speaker, and itinerant minister. Joe has also served as host and director of a weekly TV program on Israel and its history. He is the author of *Understanding Jesus* and *What Would Jesus Read?* and served as the host of Canada's longest-running daily TV show, *100 Huntley Street*. As the teaching pastor of POR-TICO Community Church in Mississauga, Ontario, Joe inspired congregants to better know Jesus and His teachings by having a deeper understanding of the world and time in which Jesus lived. Amaral founded the Christian Research Group in 2018.

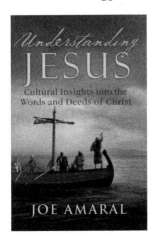
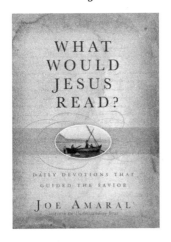